I0814625

FORMED FOR FELLOWSHIP

KYLE WORLEY

FORMED FOR FELLOWSHIP

BECOMING WHAT YOU BEHOLD

979-8-3845-2197-6

Published by B&H Publishing Group
Brentwood, Tennessee

Dewey Decimal Classification: 248.84
Subject Heading: DISCIPLESHIP / CHRISTIAN LIFE /
DISCIPLESHIP TRAINING

Cover design by B&H Publishing Group.
Author photo by Sami Kathryn Photography.

1 2 3 4 5 6 7 • 28 27 26 25

In honor of my friends, J. T. English and Jen Wilkin.
The best in this book is a fruit of our partnership and
collaboration. Brother. Sister. In Christ. Forever.

Contents

INTRODUCTION

Becoming What We Behold

I only remember one thing from high school health class. Don't judge my teacher. He was there to coach football, not teach health, and I was there to pass notes to my friends, not learn anatomy. But despite his disinterest in the subject and my distraction from it, I remember one thing he said that sounded profound at the time: "You are what you eat."

He pointed to a picture of the food pyramid (look it up if you've never heard of it—it is a *real* thing) and said, "*You are what you eat.* If you eat pizza, ice cream, and candy all day, your body will begin to look like those foods." At first, I was startled. Like almost all high school boys, my diet consisted mostly of pizza, hamburgers, soda, chips, and candy. The thought of turning into a gummy bear sounded both disastrous and delicious. But it turns out, as you might already know (because *you* listened in health class), body composition and diet are a lot more complicated than this.

For a long time, I thought "you are what you eat," was just a way to discourage us from eating too much of the wrong kinds of foods, but what very few people know is this quote did not begin its journey into our conversations as a statement about our diet—it began as a statement about our existence. Specifically, it was objecting to the Christian view of our existence. It turns out my health class had become a school of philosophy, which surely would have boggled the mind of that teacher just trying to make it to after-school practice if he had realized he stumbled upon something more fundamental than food.

The quote originates with a German philosopher named Ludwig Feuerbach, who was no fan of Christianity. Not at all. He was what we call a "materialist." He believed all we are is matter. For Feuerbach, there is nothing beyond the material world: no God, no heaven, no soul. So when he said, "Man is what he eats," he didn't mean that if you ate a donut, you'd begin to look like a donut (thank heavens!). He meant you and the donut are the same thing. You both are matter. Nothing more and nothing less.

Thankfully, Feuerbach was wrong. We aren't what we eat. We are more than matter. We humans are creatures made in the image of God, composed of body and soul. We were made with a purpose. We are not becoming what we eat, but we are becoming something. We were created to grow and change, to become.

We are born into this world not knowing who we are, but with a deep desire to become something more. We are like a toddler who doesn't know their own age but pretends to be a great lion. We enter this world not knowing what we are, who we are meant to be, and how we got here, yet absolutely certain we were meant to become something more than we are by nature.

I don't just mean we are born as infants who haven't yet developed self-awareness. That's true, but it isn't truly *the* problem. Our ignorance isn't fundamentally developmental; it goes deeper, all the way to our soul. We are born separated from who we were designed to *be*. And separated from the God who can transform us into that "something more." It's not just that we don't know who we were created to be, it's that we can't know it. Our true identity as image-bearers of God is across a great chasm we cannot cross on our own.

Because we don't know who we are, we have no clue as to what we can become. So we end up becoming the sum total of what hooks our love, desire, knowledge, and imagination. We end up looking like whatever we love. What we worship begins to work itself out in *what* we believe, *why* we think we are here, and the *way* we live.

As some have said: *we become what we behold.*

We are more changeable than we might believe. Even the most stubborn among us is constantly being shaped by who and what is around them, like a large boulder sitting in a riverbed. You may not see it over a matter of seconds, but watch that boulder for one hundred years. Then watch it for a hundred more. Bit by bit, the river shapes the boulder, cutting it back, softening the edges, and re-forming the rock.

Formation is slow, but it is constant. It never stops. We are changing—being changed—in ways we are aware of and unaware of at all times. But contrary to what some have suggested, we don't begin as blank slates. We are born into this world malformed, out of shape. We are in desperate need to be re-formed, to be re-aligned with the ways, words, and wonders of God. Why? Because God wants us to enjoy fellowship with Him, His people, and His world, but we can't do this unless we are re-formed.

Before we can become what we were always intended to be, we must be born again. Made new. Made alive. To be re-formed we have to first be transformed. This is the journey of Christian formation: becoming what we were already declared to be; becoming who we already are in Christ.

The journey of Christian formation begins, ends, and is filled with God's people beholding God.

And as we behold God, we become like Him.

CHAPTER 1

What Is a Person?

What is a human being that
you remember him,
a son of man that you look after him?
You made him little less than God
and crowned him with glory and honor.
You made him ruler over the works
of your hands;
you put everything under his feet.
Psalm 8:4–6

Walking through the park with a curious child will make you realize just how much you don't know about the world. Consider this series of questions that seem so obvious and yet the answers escape you:

- What's the sky?
- Where does the water in the toilet come from?

- What kind of tree is that?
- Who built this slide?
- Do squirrels have birthday parties?

Every question is simultaneously so simple as to be right in front of you and so complex as to make it seem like you are being quizzed about the deepest mysteries of the world. I found myself telling my brilliant little daughter "I don't know" so much that I think for a time she thought it was my name.

The most important questions we must answer to live a purposeful life, at first glance, appear to be surprisingly simple or even obvious, but we would be wrong to assume all would answer them the same way. Everyone who has ever lived is an image-bearer of God. But because sin has broken them, they are "fractured goods." Simple questions have complicated answers because we are limited and unique creatures who approach these questions with our unique limitations and perspectives.

Let me give you an example of how this works in practice. You are a person. You are a person reading this book. You and I both know you are a person, but if I asked you, "What is a person?," you'd probably stumble a bit trying to answer the question. It's what you are, but it's hard to explain. Now imagine that you were trying to answer this question in a small group of ten people and each person in that group came from a different country, was a different age, spoke a different language, and practiced a different religion.

But I have good news for you. I have a better answer than "I don't know" for these questions. I may not know the answers to my daughter's quirky questions in the park, but I do know how to help us answer the question: "What is a person?"

Before we can begin the journey of Christian formation, we have to share a common understanding of who and what we are. Why? Because how we answer will absolutely shape our answer to this question: How are we formed? *In order to get to the beauty of who we can become by grace, we have to start with the basics of what we are by nature.* This is the task of what we call "theological anthropology," and I believe it is not just crucial for understanding how we are formed; I believe it is one of the most significant topics for life in our world in this age.

A Person Is a Creature

It doesn't take much to realize people are different. I don't mean individual people are different from other people, though that is also true. I mean people are different from other kinds of things and animals. Even if some want to pretend there is no difference between humans and animals or humans and trees, we all know this is a silly lie. You might throw a birthday party for a pet, but the pet has no sense of what it means to grow older. Pets don't have midlife crises, because pets don't reflect on the meaning of life.

The Christian doesn't have to assume this difference is there; they know humans are a different kind of creature than other created things because of what God says in His Word. In Genesis 1 and 2 we discover that Adam and Eve are created in the "image of God" (Gen. 1:27–30). Adam can't find a fitting partner among the rest of the created things because there is none that is "bone of [his] bone and flesh of [his] flesh" (Gen. 2:23).

We are creatures. There is a God who created and rules over all things. And you are not Him. You are not the Creator. You are a creature. But you are different from other kinds of creatures. You are a human person—created in the image of God.

As image-bearers of God, we are embodied creatures, and while animals also have a body, it is not a body stamped with *the* image. This is the likeness of Christ into which we are made, as whole people, body included. We aren't floating souls or brains in glass bottles. We aren't tin men. We have God-designed and God-ordained bodies, and what we do with those bodies is important. God has a lot to say about what we do with our bodies, what we put into our bodies, and where our bodies should or should not go. These bodies have limits. We need sleep, but the Creator doesn't. We need food, but the Creator doesn't. We need water, the Creator doesn't. We need another differently designed body to create new life, the Creator doesn't. God has created us with limits as a signpost to us that we are fundamentally different from God, for He is limitless.

Humans aren't just embodied creatures; we are embodied creatures with souls. As image-bearers of God, we possess qualities, characteristics, and attributes that are unique to our species. There are a number of ways we are different from other creatures, but the principal thing that sets us apart as humans are our souls. It is our souls that enable us to reflect on and relate to God, ourselves, and His world differently from other creatures.

What we call soul can be referred to as *heart* or *mind*. It's the center of who we are as image-bearers of God, granting us a unique capacity to love, worship, fear, think, desire, dream, and hope that no other creature in all of creation possesses. Whether you are a pet person or not, you and I both know that no matter how smart and sweet your puppy is, he isn't sitting in the backyard at night looking up at the stars asking: "Who made all of this?" Your cat may be plotting to knock over a cup on the counter, but she's not thinking about overthrowing the government. (At least, I don't think so. Cats are a bit tricky.)

It's this God-ordained design that determines humanity's unique purpose in all of creation. A person is a creature:

created by God with a body and soul in order to behold God so that they might enjoy Him and become a reflection of His presence and purposes wherever God places them.

A Person Is Created for Fellowship

We are individuals, but we were not created to live isolated lives. Even the feeling and discouragement of loneliness is a signpost that "it is not good for the man to be alone" (Gen. 2:18). We were created for fellowship: fellowship with God, fellowship with other people, and fellowship with God's world. As image-bearers of God, we reflect the God who created us—the triune God who exists as three Persons in one essence, an unbroken eternal delighting fellowship.

Our need and desire for fellowship is not a reality of sin. We are, by design, structured for relationship. We are constructed for communion, *formed for fellowship*. God did not create the world because He was lonely. He already had perfect fellowship within Himself, needing nothing. Instead, He created out of abundant love. All creation exists out of the deliberate overflow of God's delighting fellowship. We exist out of the overflow of worship for the purpose of worship.

And yet, sin has disrupted the direction of our desire for fellowship. Rather than moving toward loving fellowship with God, we run away. Sin fractures our fellowship with God, with others, and with the natural world. Like Adam and Eve after the fall in Genesis 3, we end up trying to use God's world to hide from God's presence. Instead of looking toward God, we look away. And what we look *at* makes all the difference in what we end up looking *like*.

A Person Is Created to Behold

All the data tells us that we are born into this world looking for someone.[1] You and I are born to behold. And that's because we were *created* to behold.

To behold is more than mere seeing. I see my phone on the desk; I see the computer in front of me as I type these words; I see the limbs swaying in the breeze outside of my window. But when my wife smiled at me from across the living room this morning as I sipped coffee, my eyes had barely shaken the sleep off, but I beheld my wife. Beholding is attention that evokes devotion, delight, praise, thanksgiving, or even sorrow. You might be surprised to see sorrow included here, but we all know how easy it is to avoid bearing witness to genuine godly grief. Why does the grieving heart hide their face as they sob in their hands? To be seen in grief and to behold those in grief draws out our humanity into the realm of vulnerable love. Beholding is attention that leads to allegiance and affection.

While there are many good gifts in this world that we are invited to behold, we were created to behold God. To worship Him, to attend to His presence above and beyond any and all else. Nothing but God will ever satisfy this longing. As the writer of Ecclesiastes tells us, eternity has been placed in our hearts (Eccles. 3:11). When Jesus meets the woman at the well in Samaria, she's thirsty for something beyond what can be pulled up with a bucket. Jesus tells her, "Whoever drinks from the water that I will give him will never get thirsty again. In fact, the water I will give him will become a well of water springing up in him for eternal life" (John 4:14). She came looking for water, and Jesus invited her to behold the God who quenches our deepest thirsts.

Adam and Eve were created so that they could behold God by living their life in His presence, reflecting His purposes, in His place. God creates the world as a temple that is to be filled with the worship of God. Humanity was designed to worship God, reflect His image to the world, and bear witness throughout all of creation to His glory. The rupture in the garden has disrupted this design, but it hasn't destroyed it. When humanity rebelled against God, they fractured their fellowship with God, but they weren't forsaken by Him. We were created to behold God so we can become like God. But we need real help.

A Person Is Created to Become

I can put on a mask if I want to pretend to be a superhero, but don't ask me to fly through the air to rescue a falling child.

Even the most convincing costume won't turn me into what I look like in the mirror. It takes more than a mask to become a superhero and it takes more than a mirror to know who we were created to become.

Bookstores, social media accounts, and podcasts are full of people with a vague sense that there must be some reason why they exist. Everyone seems to be looking for help or offering up some kind of solution to the universal urge to *become*. Our culture's obsession with becoming knows no bounds: becoming healthy, becoming wealthy, becoming successful, becoming important, becoming productive, becoming valuable, becoming worthy, becoming loved. Everyone feels that they were made to be something more than what they are by nature. Why?

In the beginning, God gave humanity a purpose. He created Adam and Eve in His image, He blessed them, and He commissioned them: "Be fruitful and multiply and fill the earth and subdue it, and have dominion . . . over every living thing that moves on the earth" (Gen. 1:28 ESV). Consider for a moment that everything God commissions Adam and Eve (and with them all of humanity) to do is a reflection of what He has already done. God tells them to "be fruitful and multiply." The Creator God tells them to become creators, because He is the Creator. Their creation will be different from His; they will create from what God has already made, He created from nothing.

God tells them to "subdue and have dominion" over every living thing. The Lord God who rules over all things tells them to reign over His world. It's not their possession, they don't own it, but He is entrusting it to their stewardship. He reigns over all things, so He gives them rule over some things.

If Adam and Eve wanted to become what God was asking of them, they need only look back to God to see a picture for what it should look like. If they just kept beholding God, they would become what God was inviting them to become. But they stopped beholding God in order to try and become God. Not *like* God. They tried to become God Himself.

A Person Will Become What They Behold

We are creatures of body and soul, image-bearers of God who have been created by God in order to behold God and become a reflection of His presence and purposes. This is why we exist, but we aren't born this way. We are born as a broken reflection of this created goal. Like looking into a cracked mirror, we are left with fragments, glimpses, bits and pieces of what we were intended to reflect.

Because of sin, we are born into this world looking through fractured lenses. Have you ever tried to dive under the water with leaky goggles? For a moment it seems like you can see clearly, but once the water gets in, we might mistake a

Coke can for a clown fish. We are broken beholders, all of us by nature. Apart from God's intervention we will eventually end up giving our attention, allegiance, and affection away to idols that will promise us new beginnings, but only give new burdens.

Adam and Eve were meant to behold God and become more like Him as they lived out His purposes in the world. But shortly after they are established in God's garden, they look away from God. The temptation of the serpent in Genesis 3 is nothing less than an invitation to turn away from the trusting embrace and worship of God. But what is the central temptation in this event? "For God knows that when you eat of it your eyes will be opened, and you will be like God, knowing good and evil" (Gen. 3:5 ESV). Already made in God's image, the temptation of Satan in the garden isn't to become more like God, but to *become* God. For the creatures to become the Creator. For the stewards to become the owners.

And "when the woman saw that the tree was good for food, and that it was a delight to the eyes, and that the tree was to be desired to make one wise, she took of its fruit and ate, and she also gave some to her husband who was with her, and he ate. Then the eyes of both were opened, and they knew that they were naked. And they sewed fig leaves together and made themselves loincloths" (vv. 6–7 ESV).

God made humanity as creatures of body and soul. Consider for a moment how the temptation to become what the serpent promises involves their whole humanity. They see and hear the serpent; they trust his promise while rejecting the words of God; they behold the potential to become God; they desire a new way of living; and they act by taking the fruit and eating.

And they become something, but it is not more than what they were, it's less. Adam and Eve become what they behold in Genesis 3, and it leaves them naked and ashamed. They are exiled from the garden, and their access to the tree of life is removed, beginning the long story of exile, rescue, judgment, and redemption.

But the story doesn't end in a garden, it ends in a city. If we go all the way to the end of the story, we find a new beginning. In Revelation 22, God brings a new city to a new earth, and there is a river flowing from the throne of God. Planted by this river is the tree of life which is "for the healing of the nations" (v. 2 ESV). And then we are told: "No longer will there be anything accursed, but the throne of God and of the Lamb will be in it, and his servants will worship him. *They will see his face, and his name will be on their foreheads. And night will be no more.* They will need no light of lamp or sun, for the Lord God will be their light, and they will reign forever and ever" (vv. 3–5 ESV, emphasis added).

We were created to live as God's people in God's presence to reflect God's purposes in God's place. But the garden story ends with exile, curses, and consequences. All because our first parents became what they beheld: in an attempt to become God, they "exchanged the glory of the immortal God for images resembling mortal man and birds and animals and creeping things" (Rom. 1:23 ESV). They beheld a lesser glory and became less than what they were created to be.

And yet, when God restores the whole world, when the story is "finished," what will we discover? We find God's people in God's presence reflecting God's purposes in God's place. We will become what we behold. We were created for this, designed to begin to look like whatever we love most, to reflect in our habits what we receive in our hearts.

Becoming what we behold is how we were created to live. And it is the pattern of Christian formation.

Reflect: Why does God care about the ordinary things we do? What's something you ordinarily do that you have a hard time believing God cares about?

Discuss: If you asked one of your neighbors to define *person*, what words would they use?

Practice: Take a blank piece of paper and try to answer the question, "What/Who am I?" Don't use any words that describe what you do for work.

CHAPTER 2

How Are We Formed?

Dear friends, we are God's children now, and
what we will be has not yet been revealed.
We know that when he appears, we will be
like him because we will see him as he is.
1 John 3:2

My family likes to watch cooking shows together, and our favorite is set under a sunlit tent in the beautiful English countryside. The unique combination of delicious-looking food, fun team spirit, and endearing British accents keep us coming back season after season. In this cooking show they have a "technical" challenge every episode where the contestants are given a specific thing they have to bake. But here's the catch: they are given very little information about what it is and how to make it. They might be instructed to make a "Baked Alaska" and provided with only two or three steps on how to make this dessert. They may have never seen or heard of a "Baked Alaska" before, but now they have to make a perfect one for two very picky judges. And they have little idea where to start and what to do.

I find that many Christians feel this way when they begin to consider "becoming like God." *Wait a minute—where do I even begin? If I am a person created to behold God in order to become like God, how do I do that?* On top of the general uncertainty about where to start, there is a confusion on the goal of it all. *Why should I want to embark on this adventure? Won't it be sacrificial and costly? If God already loves me and has forgiven me, why put in all the work to try to become more like Him?*

I don't want you to feel like the contestants on that baking show. I want you to know exactly what we are talking about—exactly what God is inviting you into. So let's begin with a definition:

> *Christian formation is the journey of having our heart, mind, and strength transformed by God the Father, in Christ Jesus, through the power and presence of the Holy Spirit at work in all the ordinary affairs of our life.*

This definition can find its anchor in 1 John 3:2: "Dear friends, we are God's children now, and what we will be has not yet been revealed. We know that when he appears, we will be like him because we will see him as he is."

There is a declaration in this verse: We are God's children now. Christian formation is something that happens to Christians. God declares us as His children when we enter into union with Christ by grace through faith. We are given a new identity in Christ that cannot be changed by us or stripped from us. But for God's children, there is more to come for "what we will be has not yet been revealed." God will change His children, but into what? When Christ appears in glorious return, when we behold God in a world remade, we will be changed as we see Him.

Theologians call beholding God the "beatific vision." You might recognize the word *beatific* sounds like the word *beatitude*, and this is because they share the same root. The root word here means "blessed" or "supreme blessedness." When Jesus teaches His followers in the Sermon on the Mount—the "Beatitudes"—He is showing them the blessed way. Why can He show them this way? Because He is the blessed One. To behold God is a beatific vision, because He is the supremely blessed One, and to see Him is not only to gaze upon His blessedness, but to also receive a unique blessing in the act of beholding. This is why the psalmist can say, "Seek the Lord and his strength; seek his face always" (Ps. 105:4). Why are we to seek his face always? So that we might "gaze on the beauty of the LORD" (Ps. 27:4). The beatific vision is eschatological, which means it won't be fully realized until the end of the story in the new heavens and the new earth, but we are given foretastes throughout Scripture of what this will be like and we are instructed to pursue the Lord's presence in the present moment so that we may be made like Him.

We will become what we behold. This is the anchor and the goal of Christian formation. It is the foundation and the future. God's people are formed for fellowship with God, and as they meet with Him, He changes them more and more into His likeness. This process of formation and transformation has no end. It goes on forever as we behold God.

What Is Christian Formation?

In Deuteronomy 6 we discover the answer to the question: "*What* is Christian formation?" God is instructing His people whom He has just rescued from slavery in Egypt. He is teaching them how they are to live with God in the sight of the world. There are many commands, but one stands above and beneath them all: "Listen, Israel: The Lord our God, the Lord is one. Love the Lord your God with all your heart, with all your soul, and with all your strength" (vv. 4–5). How do we know this is the greatest command? Because Jesus expands on this in Matthew 22:36–40, "Love the Lord your God with all your heart, with all your soul, and with all your mind. This is the greatest and most important command. The second is like it: Love your neighbor as yourself. All the Law and the Prophets depend on these two commands."

Christian formation is nothing less than the journey of becoming the kind of person who increasingly loves God, neighbors, and self in ways that conform to God's Word, will, and works. When God's Word talks about loving with all our heart, soul, mind, and strength—it isn't talking about four different things. God's invitation in Deuteronomy 6 and Matthew 22 isn't into a *fractured* love, but a *full* love. This is the "what?" of Christian formation: growing into this full love, but *how*? How do we become this kind of person?

To answer the question of "how?" we turn to the Psalms. In Psalm 119:32–37 we hear the pleas of the psalmist, "I pursue the way of your commands, for you broaden my understanding. Teach me, LORD, the meaning of your statutes, and I will always keep them. Help me understand your instruction, and I will obey it and follow it with all my heart. . . . Turn my eyes from looking at what is worthless; give me life in your ways." Our eyes must be turned from looking at worthless things, to beholding the Worthy One. As the psalmist wrote in Psalm 17:15, "But I will see your face in righteousness; when I awake, I will be satisfied with your presence." We are called to "Seek his face" (Ps. 27:8). In order to become like God, we must behold God. We must pay attention to His words, we must meditate upon His wondrous works, we must look upon the Lord.

As the Lord enlarges our heart to walk in His ways, we can live like Him. We walk in His ways because He grants us the grace and power to do so. And as we walk in the ways of the Lord, we are conformed to His character. This work requires sacrifice. It is as Paul says in Romans 12:1–2 (ESV), "a living sacrifice." So, why? Why undertake this journey if you have already been forgiven? If heaven is already assured, why endeavor to "not be conformed to this world, but be transformed by the renewal of your mind"?

In 2 Corinthians 3:18 we are promised, "We all, with unveiled faces, are looking as in a mirror at the glory of the Lord and are being transformed into the same image from glory to glory; this is from the Lord who is the Spirit." This is the goal of Christian formation: to behold God forever. And in our beholding, to be changed. Over and over again. For good. Forever. As Jesus says, "Blessed are the pure in heart, for they will see God" (Matt. 5:8). This is the blessing of Aaron, "May the LORD bless you and protect you; may the LORD make his face shine on you and be gracious to you; may the LORD look with favor on you and give you peace" (Num. 6:24–26). This is the promise of heaven, "Then he showed me the river of the water of life, clear as crystal, flowing from the throne of God and of the Lamb. . . . and there will no longer be any curse. The throne of God and of the Lamb will be in the city, and his servants will worship him. They will see his face and his name will be on their foreheads. Night will be no more; people will not need the light of a lamp or the light of the sun, because the Lord God will give them light, and they will reign forever and ever" (Rev. 22:1–5).

Christian formation is a journey. It is not a "there and back again" tale, it is a "further up and further in" story.[2] It doesn't end, but it has a beginning. And in order to really understand the journey of our formation, we have to start at the beginning. Actually, we have to start *before* the beginning.

Before the Beginning of Christian Formation

You and I aren't eternal creatures. We are forever creatures. We will have no end, but we all had a beginning. There was a time in which we were not. There was a time before we existed. And before any of us showed up: There was a garden kingdom and a terrible rebellion. To make a long story short: God created the world good. He placed humanity as His "very good" creation right in the middle and entrusted the care of His garden kingdom to His people. Things were good. For a moment.

But our first parents, Adam and Eve, failed. They rebelled against God and His kingdom, disobeying His words. Because of this, everyone who has ever lived has been born into this world "in Adam." We are born guilty, sinful, and broken. You can say that we are born into this world "malformed." God tells us in Romans 3, "There is no one righteous, not even one. There is no one who understands; there is no one who seeks God" (vv. 10–11).

Al Wolters suggests that it's helpful to distinguish between the "structure" of a created thing and the "direction" of a created thing.[3] The structure of created things is what God has intended or declared something to be in His creation law. The direction of a created thing is their deviation from or alignment with God's good design. Humans were created in the image of God. We were created to reflect God in the world. And yet, we are born into this world *bent* in the wrong direction. Our structure is sound, but our direction is broken.

We do not enter this world as intended. We are born separated from God, alienated from a true knowledge of who we are, and what we were meant to be. We are born wrong, becoming something even worse. We are born with our hearts covered with hooks. These hooks will catch on to anything that promises fulfillment, identity, hope, delight, happiness, healing. And there are many stories looking to tell us a tale about who we are and how we are to live. We call these "false stories." A false story is any attempt to explain what is real, what is good, and what is beautiful that does not measure up to the Christian story.

False stories come in all shapes and sizes. They offer their own version to the big questions of life: Who am I? Where did I come from? Who or what is God? What's wrong with the world? What is my purpose here? False stories don't just offer answers, they have their own sets of practices and habits that help to reinforce our belief and participation in them. And they can be very tempting.

Here are some common false stories that we can fall into believing and participating in:

- Individualism: I am the center.
- Naturalism: This world is all there is.
- Rationalism: I am the measure.
- Cynicism: This world is hopeless.
- Consumerism: I am what I possess.
- Romanticism: I feel therefore I am.[4]

We are story-soaked creatures. As Alasdair MacIntyre has said, "I can only answer the question, 'What am I to do?' if I can answer the prior question, 'What story am I in?'"[5] These stories are more than just make-believe, nursery rhymes, or fiction; these stories are what we call "metanarratives." They are stories that seek to convince us of what is true, good, and beautiful. All metanarratives provide a set of answers to the big questions, and many of them will provide habits, practices, and ways of participating that pull us further up and further into those stories. False stories do exactly this.

We are born into this world living in a sin-shaped story. It may play out in one of many different false stories, but at its bedrock, all of our stories begin in the same place: in Adam—broken by sin—subject to death—citizens in a kingdom of darkness. Along the way, we are hooked by all kinds of false stories that will form us and shape us into their image. Sin has bent our sexual desires, and pornography grabs these hooks and leads many by the nose. Our attention craves distraction, gratification, and entertainment, so social media is engineered to steal our attention away from what matters most and give it to what matters least. We know we need a hero, a deliverer, so our allegiance is co-opted by every new political messiah promising us safety.

We are born into the world ready to be formed. The problem is that we are not ready to be formed into what is true, good, and beautiful. We are born malformed, prepared to be misdirected by false stories. This is why before we begin the *journey* of Christian formation, we must experience the *event* of Christian transformation.

The Beginning of Christian Formation

In high school I drove a baby blue 1954 Chevy truck. It was gorgeous. But it was also a money pit. Old cars need lots of help to keep running. And my baby blue sweetheart needed a lot of love. One day we had it out in the driveway after the whole engine had been pulled out and was getting worked on, but it looked beautiful in the summer sun. I had just got done washing and waxing it when a neighbor walked up and said, "Wow, it looks incredible. Can you take me for a spin?" I had to explain that even though the outside of the truck looked vibrant, there was no engine. The truck looked alive, but it was actually dead. It looked like it could move, but it was stuck still.

We can't start to live life with God *like* Christ until we have been made alive by God *in* Christ. Christian formation begins with the event of transformation. We can't be re-formed until we have been transformed. We actually see a wonderful summary of this transformation to formation story in Ephesians 2:1–10: "And you were dead in your trespasses and sins in which you previously walked according to the ways of this world, according to the ruler of the power of the air, the spirit now working in the disobedient. . . . But God, who is rich in mercy, because of his great love that he had for us, made us alive with Christ even though we were dead in trespasses. . . . For you are saved by grace through faith, and this is not from yourselves; it is God's gift—not from works, so that no one can boast. For we are his workmanship, created in Christ Jesus for good works, which God prepared ahead of time for us to do."

We've already discussed the bad news. You and I are born busted, "dead in our trespasses and sins." But here is the good news: God, because of His great love and mercy, makes "us alive with Christ." And this is all "God's gift." It's on the foundation of this new life we are given in Christ that we are released to practice the "good works, which God prepared ahead of time for us to do." We are born into this world malformed by sin, but God transforms by grace through faith in Christ, so we can embark on the journey of Christian formation by walking in what God has prepared.

In salvation, our heart of stone is replaced with a heart of flesh (Ezek. 36:26), we move from death to life (Rom. 6:1–4), we are transferred from the kingdom of darkness into God's kingdom (Col. 1:13–14). This is the beginning of salvation, but it is not the end. The goal of salvation isn't forgiveness; it's freedom for fellowship with God. This is the path and destination of Christian formation: fellowship with the living God who has redeemed us in His Son. But the only way we can walk in this path is by the grace of God and the power of the Holy Spirit.

The Engine of Christian Formation

After we have been transformed by God's grace, we continue on the journey of Christian formation empowered by God's grace. We don't undertake or complete the journey on our own power, but we do actively participate in this journey of formation in a way that we could never have participated before the transformation of our salvation in Christ. To say it simply: the transformation of Christian salvation does not include any of our participation, but the journey of Christian formation involves our actions.

We get a sense of this profound tension between what God is doing in and through us and what we are doing in our ordinary lives when Paul says that he labors toward what God has called him to "striving with his strength that works powerfully in me" (Col. 1:29). This is a great way to capture the engine of Christian formation: God works His strength within us. So our striving, our obedience, our faithfulness is made possible and made powerful by the indwelling Spirit of God, who is "the down payment of our inheritance, until the redemption of the possession, to the praise of his glory" (Eph. 1:14).

Make no mistakes about what I mean: God is the principal power at work in our sanctification and Christian formation. We cannot become like God; there is no transformation of our character apart from His power and presence at work in our lives. The glory and the credit belong to Him. We can trust that "he who started a good work in you will carry it on to completion until the day of Christ Jesus" (Phil. 1:6). This is good news. God is going to keep us and keep working in us all the way to the end of the journey. And at the same time, what are we to do with all the power God has provided us in Christ and by the work of the Holy Spirit? We are to "pursue peace with everyone, and holiness—without it no one will see the Lord" (Heb. 12:14).

How does God lead us in this path? By the indwelling power of the Holy Spirit. Apart from the work of the Holy

Spirit, there is no possibility that we may be formed to look like Christ. In this book we will discuss "formative practices" we can engage in to pursue change, but these practices are worthless apart from the work of the Holy Spirit. It is the One who has begun a good work in us that is faithful to bring it to completion. We are only able to become like God because God's Spirit resides in us.

The Journey of Christian Formation

It has become fashionable to say something like this when explaining the gospel: "The gospel doesn't make bad people good, it makes dead people alive." Spoiler: I don't like this phrasing. The good news of the gospel is that God makes dead people alive. And having made them alive, He begins to make bad people good. It is good news that we aren't just made alive by God in Christ, but that God begins to make us look and live like Christ. But, how? How does God make us look and live like Christ?

As image-bearers of God, we are creatures of body and soul. We are not purely material. We are spirit and body. We are not just what we eat. We are creatures who think, feel, desire, love, worship, dream, and act. And all of this happens in, with, and through bodies designed by our Creator. We are embodied creatures who are more (but not less!) than our bodies. The God who created us is the God who redeems us in Christ and the very same God who forms us into becoming like Christ. He knows how we change; He made us.

God transforms our heart, mind, and strength in Christ Jesus through the power and presence of the Holy Spirit at work in all the ordinary affairs of our life—the places we live, the people we live among, what we love, what we think about, what we do, how we use our time, what has our attention. We get a taste of this in Paul's words in 1 Corinthians 10:31–11:1, "So, whether you eat or drink, or whatever you do, do everything for the glory of God. . . . Imitate me, as I also imitate Christ."

What a wonderfully ordinary way to give glory to God. Right before Paul tells them, "Imitate me, as I also imitate Christ," he reminds them that they can honor God with what and how they chew and sip. Christian formation is as ordinary as eating and drinking. But for many Christians, they don't know where to start. They have a desire to have their hearts, mind, and strength formed into the likeness of Christ, but they aren't sure where to begin.

Some might imagine the Christian life is like getting into a parked car. They believe God wants them to sit there until He tells them exactly where to go, what speed to drive, and how to get there. God does guide us in the journey of Christian formation, but it is far less robotic than we often think. We aren't placed in a parked car and told to sit and wait for further instruction. We are invited to get moving through all the ordinary affairs of life with an attention given to the presence of God "in him we live and move and have our being" (Acts 17:28).

A significant part of the journey of Christian formation includes what have been called by many the spiritual disciplines. Among these "spiritual disciplines" we often find prayer, worship, study, fasting, meditation. We shouldn't be surprised to discover that Christian formation involves doing things. As we have already discovered, as embodied creatures, we are shaped by what we do and by what we don't do. The spiritual disciplines don't change and shape you because they are some kind of secret code word you have to whisper to be received at God's front door. They shape you because everything you do shapes you. Even what you eat and drink.

In this book, we will refer to the "spiritual disciplines" as "formative practices." Why? For two reasons:

1. Calling these practices "spiritual disciplines" often neglects that they aren't purely spiritual—they take place in our embodied lives with other embodied people.
2. These habits are for the purpose of formation. They aren't disciplines we undertake purely for the sake of duty. They are not aimed at self-improvement, but at becoming who God has designed us to be.

These formative practices are not just random. They are rooted and grounded in the character and works of God. This will be my main point in this book: **The journey of Christian formation is a journey of becoming what we behold. God calls us to these specific practices specifically because they are reflections of His nature and work.** The habits and practices of the Christian life are meant to form the way that our faith in God shapes our ordinary lives. We will explore each "formative practice" by beginning with the nature, character, words, and works of God. Only when we are sure that we are looking at God instead of looking at ourselves will we have any degree of confidence that we can begin to look like God.

This is a common pitfall with much of the literature on "spiritual disciplines." The focus shifts to the self: *What do I need to do? What can I do?* But that misses the point entirely: Christian formation doesn't begin and end with you looking deeper into yourself—it begins and ends with you looking at God.

The Community of Christian Formation

The journey of Christian formation is personal, but it is not private. When we experience Christian transformation, we are welcomed into new life in God's Spirit–indwelt family in Christ. This means we don't just receive the formative fellowship of God; we now belong to a community of others who are being formed by the presence and purposes of God. This formative community is called the church. You might say that "in Christ" we don't just become a "new me," we receive a "new we." God forms us for fellowship with Him as we fellowship with His people.

We do not undertake the journey of Christian formation alone. As God said in the garden, "It is not good for the man to be alone" (Gen. 2:18). This holds true throughout God's story and comes to its proper fulfillment in the body of Christ. Every local church is a visible expression of the larger body of Christ. The church is a formative community that encourages, supports, and challenges its members to continue along the path of holiness, to continue pursuing Christ-likeness. We aren't just story shaped-creatures; we are creatures made for community.

It is telling that when most people think of spiritual formation or "spiritual disciplines," the picture that comes to mind is of a person by themselves with their Bible in the early hours of the morning with a cup of coffee. Now don't get me wrong—reading your Bible is great. Getting up early is great. Coffee is great. Certainly God is shaping us into His likeness as we take time of quiet solitude with His Word open in front of us—this is wonderfully true. But I think we might be in danger of having an overly individualized view of how God shapes His people. The pattern of beholding and becoming, the formative practices we will explore throughout this book, and the entire journey of having our heart, mind, and strength transformed by God in Christ through the power and presence of the Holy Spirit will be most fruitful when embedded within meaningful participation in the church.

Consider for a moment that when God rescues Israel from Egypt He tells them in Exodus 19, "Now therefore, if you will indeed obey my voice and keep my covenant, you shall be my treasured possession among all peoples, for all the earth is mine; and you shall be to me a kingdom of priests and a holy nation" (vv. 5–6 ESV). When the church is born at Pentecost in Acts 2 we are told that "they devoted themselves to the apostles' teaching and the fellowship, to the breaking of bread and the prayers. . . . And all who believed were together and had all things in common. . . . And day by day, attending the temple together and breaking bread in their homes, they received their food with glad and generous hearts, praising God and having favor with all the people. And the Lord added to their number day by day those who were being saved" (vv. 42–47 ESV). Notice the language here: "they . . . were together . . . in common . . . attending together." God's work of forming His people more and more into His likeness is embedded in His created and redeemed community.

The journey of Christian formation is not meant to be undertaken alone. God uses the fellowship, worship, devotion, and practices of His people to form each person that belongs to Him in Christ.

The Goal of Christian Formation

Let's imagine your friend asks you to come over to their house to help them with a backyard project. When you arrive you discover shovels, wheelbarrows, and a giant pile of rocks in the corner of their yard. Don't lie—you are immediately regretting your offer to help. You and your friend begin moving the rocks. It's hard work. The summer sun is hot. Your friend tells you to move the rocks to the other side of the yard. It feels meaningless. You are literally just shoveling and moving rocks from one place to the next. You start to get frustrated: "Why are we doing this? What's the point?"

You finish the project and clear that corner of the yard of all the rocks. Your friend looks at you and says, "We are almost done." You finally lose your cool: "Almost done! We've been working all day to clear the rocks. Moving them from one corner to the next. I am dead tired. Why are we doing all of this?" Your friend picks up a shovel and says, "About two feet under our feet is a treasure chest full of gold and diamonds. I figured I'd split it with you." Two questions: Do you pick up the shovel and finish the job? Do you now look back on all that work you've done differently than you had a few moments before?

The journey of Christian formation is costly. The formative practices of prayer, meditation on God's Word, holy obedience, sacrificial love will be challenging in a broken world.

It is hard work to pursue holiness; it can be lonely to love the hard-to-love; it isn't always sweet to serve. But there is a treasure chest just beneath our feet. We might not always see it in the present moment, but the goal of Christian formation is greater joy with God as we become more aligned with His character, His purposes, and His will.

Why embark on the journey of Christian formation? So that you might be formed into the kind of person who enjoys God here and now, reflects God in the life of the world, and is eager to experience the blessings of forever fellowship with God in the life to come. "Dear friends, we are God's children now, and what we will be has not yet been revealed. We know that when he appears, we will be like him because we will see him as he is" (1 John 3:2). What God has declared us to be, His children, will never change. But He is inviting us to increasingly become what He has already declared us to be. He is inviting us to behold who He has always been, so that we might become who we were designed and delivered to be. God is forming us so that we might enjoy the blessing of fellowship with God and fellowship with His people.

For the remainder of the book, we are going to look at the "formative practices" of the Christian life. In each chapter, we will begin with beholding. Every practice on the road of Christian formation is first an opportunity to behold who God is and what He has done. Only once we have looked at God can we begin to look *like* God. The way we have been created by God and the entire story of Scripture testify that we will become what we behold.

And so we begin by beholding God's invitation to live *with* Him by living *in* Him.

A Brief Note on Suffering and Christian Formation

Before we move further into our exploration of Christian formation, I need to pause here to talk about suffering. It is indisputable that God forms His people as they undergo suffering. Romans 5:3–5, "And not only that, but we also boast in our afflictions, because we know that affliction produces endurance, endurance produces proven character, and proven character produces hope. This hope will not disappoint us, because God's love has been poured out in our hearts through the Holy Spirit who was given to us."

While it is often true that we would rather God shape us using any other means but suffering, all throughout Scripture and in the witness of the church we discover that God uses suffering and affliction to shape His people. When we are formed through suffering, we experience a unique connection with the life and work of Christ, in whose image we are being shaped.

Since the focus of this book is the formative practices we can undertake, there is not an extended treatment of suffering. We don't pursue the practice of suffering. But as God's people undergo trials, God is shaping and forming us. This book is an encouragement to reflect on God as you undertake the habits of "drawing near to God."

Reflect: Where do we find examples of beholding God's glory (shadows of the beatific vision), throughout the story of Scripture?

Discuss: How do people throughout Scripture respond when they encounter the glory of God? How does it change them?

Practice: Do a sketch of your life story. Try to keep it to one page, but jot down the major people, places, and events that come to mind. Think about the major disappointments and high points along the way. Imagine your life as a book, a movie, a play: Who are the characters? What are the chapters or scenes? Describe the setting. Don't worry too much about all the chronological details. Pay special attention to the things that have "shaped" you the most. After you finish, take some time to share it with a trustworthy person in your life.

CHAPTER 3

Where Do We Belong?

For by one offering he has perfected
forever those who are being sanctified.
Hebrews 10:14

We have a flowerpot in the backyard. Don't be impressed. The "weed sanctuary" would be a more accurate name for what it has become. And let me tell you something you already know: you can't grow cookies in that flowerpot. I haven't tried to plant cookies in there, but I know enough to know that if I bury a couple of snickerdoodles in the backyard, all I'm going to grow is ant piles.

In order for something or someone to thrive and flourish, they have to be rooted in the right kind of soil, into where it belongs. The only question is "where?" When God created the world, He created the world so that His people could live their whole lives in His presence in His place to reflect His purposes. And even though sin has disrupted our fellowship with God, nothing has changed about where we are meant to live. The good news of the gospel is that God has invited us into His fellowship, into life with Him, through the work of Christ (Heb. 10:19–25).

We are created to live with God in Christ. God designed us for fellowship, but we are born into the world forsaken. Fellowship with God is the only place where we will grow the right fruit. Cookies won't grow in gardens, and Christians won't grow outside of Christ. In Christian doctrine, this reality is captured best in the doctrine of union with Christ and communion with God. As I have written elsewhere, Christ is where we are invited to receive our home with God.[6] In our union with Christ, we are welcomed into God's unbreakable and unshakable fellowship. We inhabit Christ and can never be evicted. In Christ, we receive a new identity as children of God that cannot be stripped away.

Why is this crucial to understand for the journey of Christian formation? We can only grow into becoming more like God when we are grounded in beholding the God of the gospel. And we will only be able to *behold* the God of the gospel when we have come to *belong* to the God of the gospel.

When we behold God's welcome in Christ, we will become people who increasingly look like Him.

God Is Gracious

God welcomes us to make our home with Him. He doesn't have to do this. We are not born into this world entitled to God's love. His love is gracious—it is undeserved. We enter this world with homeless hearts, but God invites us to live with Him. The home He provides is where we can grow up into looking more and more like God.

Throughout the entire story of Scripture, from the garden in Genesis all the way to the city in Revelation, we discover that "God's dwelling is with humanity, and he will live with them. They will be his peoples, and God himself will be with them and will be their God" (Rev. 21:3). The grace of God greets His people at the front door of life with Him.

As Paul writes in Ephesians 2:1–10, we enter this world "dead in your trespasses and sins." But because of God's gracious love and His rich mercy, He makes "us alive with Christ even though we were dead in trespasses. You are saved by grace!" The grace of God transforms us from death to life. Before we can live with God, we must be made alive by God. But this isn't the only transformation God's grace accomplishes. Paul continues in this passage, "For you are saved by grace through faith, and this is not from yourselves; it is God's gift—not from works, so that no one can boast. For we are his workmanship, created in Christ Jesus for good works, which God prepared ahead of time for us to do" (vv. 8–10).

The grace of God *transforms* before it *forms.* It transforms us from death to life, then it begins to form us into the kind of people who can live in God's ways. God's grace makes us alive, then it empowers and sustains our living. His grace saves us and sanctifies us. God's grace welcomes us into His fellowship and sustains us as we answer His call to follow in His ways. What does this mean? There is no living like Jesus until we have received new life in Jesus.

And all of this is grace. Every bit of it. As Paul reminds us in another letter: "For the grace of God has appeared, bringing salvation for all people, instructing us to deny godlessness and worldly lusts and to live in a sensible, righteous, and godly way in the present age, while we wait for the blessed hope, the appearing of the glory of our great God and Savior, Jesus Christ" (Titus 2:11–13). The flow of this passage is a picture to us of the whole Christian life. Salvation has come for all and it carries with it a purpose: "instructing us to deny godlessness and worldly lusts and to live in a . . . godly way in the present age."

Make no mistake about it. Hear me loud and clear right at the beginning of this book: It is God's grace that empowers and works to form us into the image of Christ. Grace, not grit, is the foundation of all Christian formation. God's grace, administered in Christ Jesus, by the power of the Holy Spirit. Even in our efforts to pursue Christ-likeness we strive "in his strength" (Col. 1:29) that powerfully works within us. The entire journey of Christian formation is undertaken on pathways paved with grace.

This is the journey of Christian formation: God's people transformed in Christ so that they may live obedient to God while we wait for the return of King Jesus. And this journey begins with belonging.

We Belong in Christ

Let's imagine you need a place to live. You have fallen on hard times and have nowhere to go. One day we meet; I hear your story and invite you to come and live with me. I have plenty of room and offer you a place to stay. I tell you to come by anytime, and I'll have a private room set aside for you. What's the one thing you absolutely have to ask before you and I go our separate ways? "Where do you live?" If you don't know how to get to my home, then the invitation to live with me is a bit hollow.

If God's grace invites us to live with Him, what's the address of His home? Simply: Christ Jesus. This reality is called "union with Christ." When God invites us to live *with* Him, we receive this invitation by placing our faith *in* Him. And in this union with Christ we are now the recipients of God's unbreakable covenant love and we are filled with the power and presence of the Holy Spirit.

The journey of Christian formation is undertaken day in and day out on a remarkably secure foundation: a home with God that can never be lost. In Christ, God gives a new identity, a new people, and a new way to live. These gifts cannot ever be lost by us, because they are not kept by us. God keeps these gifts for us in Christ Jesus. Where He keeps His people, for good, forever. This means that we can undertake the adventure of pursuing Christ's better way, knowing that if we fail, we will fail into a home that we can never lose. The Father will never kick us to the curb. Why? How can we live with God in Christ if we are born into this world separated from Him by sin? Because Christ Jesus, the Son of God, was forsaken by the Father so that we could enjoy fellowship with Him. It is because Christ was condemned that we can have communion with God.

Nothing can disrupt our union with Christ. Nothing can pull us away from God's love for His children. As we hear in Paul's letter to the church in Rome, "For I am persuaded that neither death nor life, nor angels nor rulers, nor things present nor things to come, nor powers, nor height nor depth, nor any other created thing will be able to separate us from the love of God that is in Christ Jesus our Lord" (Rom. 8:38–39). We must behold this wonderful reality. We can't miss it, because if we do, we will undertake the "formative practices" of the Christian life with the desire to gain God's favor. But we don't chase after conformity to Christ to try and prove that we belong. In Christ, we have nothing left to prove. It is from this new identity that we can boldly step into the adventure of abiding.

If we miss the startling reality of union with Christ, we will chase becoming like God in order that we might be loved by God. But this isn't the gospel. In the gospel, God invites us into life with Him before we resemble Him at all. It is only after we receive God's invitation into life in Christ by grace through faith that we can become people who increasingly reflect Him. The most fundamental and ordinary thing that can be said about a Christian is that they are someone who now, because of God's grace, belongs to God in Christ Jesus. And nothing can change that.

But even after we are invited to live at home with God, we often choose lesser things. We hear God's invitation to come and live in Christ, but we choose to sleep on an empty bench in the park, rather than receive the home prepared for us. We know that belonging requires surrender and we are desperate to not give ourselves up. To gain our lives we must lose them. We have to die in order to live. Once we are welcomed into God's home, we are still tempted to forsake that home like the prodigal son and end up eating slop with the pigs. Thinking to ourselves, *At least I'm still in control.* But the road to freedom with God begins by surrendering the illusion of control for the joy of fellowship with God. In order to receive a new home with God, we have to be willing to drop the cosplay of control.

We Belong with God

Our union with Christ is our home with God. For those in Christ Jesus, God will never forsake them, God will never lose them, and God will be faithful to them forever. Our union with Christ is unbreakable and unshakable. But our communion with God can be deepened, disrupted, broken, shaken, and strengthened. Our communion with God is our experience of all the blessings and conformity to all the purposes God has secured for us as His people in Christ Jesus.

We belong with God in Christ Jesus. In our life with God, every day is an opportunity for spiritual growth and maturity. Every day we are presented with a question: Will we be formed into greater likeness with the God who loves us unconditionally? Or, will we behold lesser gods and gifts and become something else? In other words: Will we become what God has already declared us to be?

In Hebrews 10:14 we hear, "For by one offering [Christ] has perfected forever those who are being sanctified." In this one verse we are struck by the glorious tension of the Christian life: With God in Christ, I am declared perfect. With God in Christ, I am being made perfect. With God in Christ, I will be made perfect. To be sanctified is to be brought into alignment with the purposes and character of God and His kingdom. This happens for all of God's people in Christ Jesus.

We participate in this work of sanctification. God is gracious in Christ to give us a new heart that is able to listen to Him, speak with Him, worship Him, love Him, and obey Him. With this new heart, we can either choose to submit sacrificial and joyful obedience to God, or we can choose to turn our worship, loves, and submission to lesser glories. What we do here won't determine how much God loves us, but it will determine how much we resemble the God who will never stop loving us in Christ Jesus.

In John 15, Jesus captures the dynamic of life with God as He talks about the vine and branches. God's people, those in Christ Jesus, are told, "Remain in my love. If you keep my commands you will remain in my love, just as I have kept my Father's commands and remain in his love" (v. 9–10). If we aren't careful, we can read this passage and come away thinking: *I guess the only way I can belong to God is if I am perfectly obedient.* But this isn't the case. Jesus isn't telling His disciples that they will only be kept by God if they keep God's commands with perfect obedience. He's telling them if they want to experience all that God has given them freely for good forever, then obedience is the way. As He goes on to say, "I have told you these things so that my joy may be in you and your joy may be complete" (v. 11).

When we engage in formative practices, when we walk in obedience to God's commands, we put ourselves under streams of sanctifying grace that will gradually begin to form and shape us into people who can more readily receive the joy of God's love and reflect His character.

Behold/Become

My daughter talks to babies in funny voices. She has these little phrases that she uses as she speaks to them in baby talk. But I don't have to look far to find out where she learned to speak to babies like this; my wife speaks to babies in the same voices, using the same little phrases. My daughter has learned to love babies like my wife has, because my daughter lives her life with my wife.

When we behold God's invitation into life with Him, when we receive this invitation in Christ Jesus, it becomes possible to learn to look like the God we now live with. Not only is this increasing resemblance to our God and Savior possible, it is expected. The New Testament is clear that a Christian who bears no resemblance to Christ is strange—so strange that the individual should begin to ask themselves: *Am I just playing games?*

Consider what John says in 1 John, "God is light, and there is absolutely no darkness in him. If we say, 'We have fellowship with him,' and yet we walk in darkness, we are lying and not practicing the truth. . . . My little children, I am writing you these things so that you may not sin. But if anyone does sin, we have an advocate with the Father—Jesus Christ the righteous one" (1 John 1:5; 2:1). I have to admit: I treasure this passage. It captures the beautiful tension of God's welcome *and* God's warning. John is telling his audience that it is good for them to not sin. Obedience to God is good. We should pursue obedience and conformity to God. We should look to live like God as we live with God in Christ. We can and we should avoid sin. But if we do sin, God will never kick us out of His home. Why? Because we are in Christ Jesus, our advocate.

Resemblance to God in Christ and alignment with His ways is the goal of Christian formation. *Christian formation is the journey of having our heart, mind, and strength transformed by God the Father, in Christ Jesus, through the power and presence of the Holy Spirit at work in all the ordinary affairs of our life.* Our formation is a Spirit-wrought effort in Jesus: "Are you so foolish? After beginning by the Spirit, are you now finishing by the flesh?" (Gal. 3:3). We don't do this great work by our own power, but we strive "with his strength that works powerfully in me" (Col. 1:29). This is why the formative practices of the Christian life must be grounded in beholding God. He is the goal and the glory.

We begin the journey of Christian formation by beholding the God who welcomes us into life with Him in Christ. Only when we have received this invitation can we become people who reflect His character in all the ordinary affairs of life. In Christ Jesus, we are beloved by God because we are "in the Beloved One" (Eph. 1:6). And it is in beholding the "Beloved One" that we increasingly become people who are marked by love.

Reflect: Before you became a Christian, where did you look for a place to belong? What guided how you identified yourself?

Discuss: What's one area of your life God has changed and is changing you in Christ?

Practice: Get a piece of paper out and write down the two prompts below. Fill in the space after the first prompt with what was true of you when you were still defined by separation from God. For the second prompt, include something that is true of you now that you are in Christ.

- Because I was born in Adam, ______________________________.
- Because I have been born again in Christ, ______________________________.

we share with God. Even though we share these communicable attributes with God, we do not possess them in the same way He does. We can love, but God *is* love. We can know truth, but God *is* truth. We can pursue holiness, but God *is* holy. God doesn't merely possess or reflect the perfection of all good things; He *is* the perfection of all good things. This is why it is necessary to look at God if we want to reflect God. He is the substance, we are the shadow.

In 1 John 4, the apostle John reveals just how closely connected God's love is with God's nature and our practice of love. "Dear friends, let us love one another, because love is from God, and everyone who loves has been born of God and knows God. The one who does not love does not know God, because God is love. . . . Love consists in this: not that we loved God, but that he loved us and sent his Son to be the atoning sacrifice for our sins. Dear friends, if God loved us in this way, we also must love one another. . . . And we have come to know and to believe the love that God has for us. God is love, and the one who remains in love remains in God, and God remains in him. . . . We love because he first loved us" (1 John 4:7–8, 10–11, 16, 19).

Our practice of love is rooted in our reception of love from God. The love we receive from God is not a gift God pulls from outside of Himself, but rather, the deliberate overflow of who God is. If we are to reflect God's love, we must first receive God's love. A glass can only spill what it contains.

The only proper foundation of our love for anything and anyone is God's love. Every other love is sinking sand.

What Is Love?

How old were you when you discovered that the "heart" shape we draw as kids and the box we fill up with chocolates once a year actually bears no resemblance to what the actual heart in our body looks like? Maybe some of you are learning about this right now. If so, I'm not too far away from you. This is not a joke: I was eighteen years old when I sat in a college biology class and the professor put up a picture of the Valentine's heart and said, "Many people think this is what a heart looks like." Everyone in the class laughed. And I sat there thinking, *What's funny?*

The heart we draw on love letters is certainly prettier to look at, but it's not real. Sorry to pop your pretty pink balloons. In a similar way, we often settle for a picture of love that is far from the real thing. Because we are embodied creatures who think, feel, and worship, we shouldn't be surprised that love engages our emotions, our thoughts, and our desires. It's easy to say love is more than a feeling. It certainly is, but it's not less than a feeling.

So what is love? *True love is rightly ordered devotion and desire aimed at God, others, and self (in that order).* Ultimately, the definition of love must be God-shaped. God shows and tells us who to love and how to love. We are invited to love and we are commanded to love. True love always involves giving ourselves away. It is always a surrender of self. Surrendering our time, surrendering our attention, surrendering our preferences, surrendering our desires; all of this is included in the practice of love.

Jesus tells the crowds in Mark 12:30–31, "Love the Lord your God with all your heart, with all your soul, with all your mind, and with all your strength. . . . Love your neighbor as yourself. There is no command greater than these." Don't mistake what Jesus is saying: He isn't splitting up the human person into parts. He's saying: Love with all you are, love with all you have; faithful love is a fully engaged love—a whole person love. Christian love isn't some malnourished form of love; it's a fully embraced, fully formed love for God, others, and ourselves.

Jesus wasn't just giving us a definition of love; He also provides the right order of our loves: God, others, ourselves. The love of God is **worship**. God alone is worthy of our worship, praise, and adoration. Our fundamental allegiance, affection, and assent belongs to God. To give it to any other person or thing is to create an idol. Only God gets the position of highest and first love for us.

The love of others is **work**. It is challenging to love other people because we are broken and they are broken. To love others requires sacrifice, service, and self-denial. Whether they are our spouse, child, friend, family member, neighbor, or enemy; to love any other person requires laying your desires and preferences down.

The love of self feels **wrong**. I thought I was supposed to "lay my life down"? I thought I was supposed to "pick up my cross and die"? How am I supposed to love myself? We are not supposed to love who we are by nature, but we are invited to love who God declares us to be in Christ. We can't practice love for others if we hate God, and we can't practice true love for others if we hate who God has made and redeemed us to be in Christ Jesus. This is not the false self-love of the world that places the self at the center of the story. The world says: Love who you are by nature. God says: Receive your beloved identity in Christ.

Love is a key practice of Christian formation. We cannot become like God if we do not love. But *how* do we love?

How Do We Love?

I think if we are honest, we would all say that we need a "Dummy's Guide to Love." The reason we keep watching the same romantic comedies over and over is because they all capture the universal human experience of fumbling the practice of love. Almost everyone is convinced that we should love, but very rarely does anyone teach us how. So how do we practice true love? As we behold the God who is love, we become people who can love with our works, our words, and our wonder.

Love involves our **works**. Love is a verb. It requires practice and doing. If I say I love something or someone, it reshapes how I love. If I told you "I love God," but I never listen to His words, would you believe me? If I told you "I love my daughter," but I never spend time with her, would you believe me? If I told you "I love hot dogs," but I only eat hamburgers, would you believe me? You get the point. Any claim to love is hollow if it's not backed up by the way we live.

When Jesus reflects on the nature of love in John 15, He says, "This is my command: Love one another as I have loved you. No one has greater love than this: to lay down his life for his friends" (vv. 12–13). It is the love of God the Father that stands behind the sending of God the Son to rescue the world. The saving works of God are grounded in God's love. So too, our practice of true love will involve working, willing, and doing. Love is practiced in the actions of our lives. There is no such thing as a love without works.

Love influences our **words**. We talk about what we love, we talk with the people we love, we speak what is true *with* and *in* love. To practice true love will re-form our language. We are told, "Out of the abundance of the heart his mouth speaks" (Luke 6:45 ESV). Paul exhorts the church to speak "the truth in love" (Eph. 4:15). Love and language are joined at the hip. If you love something or someone, you talk about it or them. If you love a person, you speak to them.

Consider that in 1 Corinthians 13, the "love" chapter, we are told that "love is not boastful . . . is not rude . . . rejoices in the truth." If my speech is boastful, rude, and deceptive, then my language is not marked by love. As James writes, "With the tongue we bless our Lord and Father, and with it we curse people who are made in God's likeness. Blessing and cursing come out of the same mouth. My brothers and sisters, these things should not be this way" (James 3:9–10).

Love engages our **wonder**. Our desires, our dreams, our hopes, and our concerns are tied to our loves. Whatever we love will lead our longings. If you tie your love to money, you will dream of riches and you will hold back generosity. If you tie your love to achievement, you will dream of success and you will exhaust yourself with striving. Our longing is rooted in our loves. This is why we have to begin with love when considering the formative practices. If our loves are not properly ordered, then truly there will be no desire for or delight in holy matters. Anytime we begin to grow apathetic in our life with God, we should look under the hood of our loves to see what's out of alignment. When our loves are in the right order, we don't have to break our backs trying to convince ourselves to want what God says is best.

Some people and things are easy to love. You may not find it easy to love professional wrestling like me, but I bet you find it easy to love something silly too. It's not hard for me to love my daughter. It can be a bit harder to love my friends, but my friends aren't as hard to love as my enemies. Jesus tells us, "Love the Lord your God with all your heart, with all your soul, and with all your mind. This is the greatest and most important command. The second is like it: Love your neighbor as yourself. All the Law and the Prophets depend on these two commands" (Matt. 22:37–40).

St. Augustine knew something about how tricky it was to love the right things in the right way. In one of his most famous works, *On Christian Doctrine*, he says, "But living a just and holy life requires one to be capable of an objective and impartial evaluation of things: to love things, that is to say, in the right order, so that you do not love what is not to be loved, or fail to love what is to be loved, or have a greater love for what should be loved less, or an equal love for things that should be loved less or more, or a lesser or greater love for things that should be loved equally."[7] God is love. Perfect love. It's who God is. But our loves are in need of formation. We are prone to "wander." Prone to "leave the God we love." It is easy for us to settle for loving unlovely things, to love things beyond what they deserve, to love things below what they deserve. But the antidote to this isn't more attention on ourselves, it's to turn our attention to God.

Behold/Become

Why must Christian formation begin with love? Because Christian salvation begins with love. John 3:16, "For God loved the world in this way: He gave his one and only Son, so that everyone who believes in him will not perish but have eternal life." First John 4:19–21,

> We love because he first loved us. If anyone says, "I love God," and yet hates his brother or sister, he is a liar. For the person who does not love his brother or sister whom he has seen cannot love God whom he has not seen. And we have this command from him: The one who loves God must also love his brother and sister.

Love is the fundamental formative practice of the Christian life. It is at the beginning and the end of the Christian journey of beholding God and becoming like Him. Many are familiar with Paul's "love chapter" in 1 Corinthians 13, but we often overlook how our practice of love is tied to beholding God. Read carefully:

> For we know in part, and we prophesy in part, but when the perfect comes, the partial will come to an end. When I was a child, I spoke like a child, I thought like a child, I

> reasoned like a child. When I became a man, I put aside childish things. For now we see only a reflection as in a mirror, but then face to face. Now I know in part, but then I will know fully, as I am fully known. Now these three remain: faith, hope, and love—but the greatest of these is love. (1 Cor. 13:9–13)

Did you see it? Paul points the Christian to the future hope of seeing God. Right now we don't see God as clearly as we one day will, but one day we will behold Him "face to face." So what? As we know God fully and are fully known by God, what does that provoke in the life of the Christian? "Faith, hope, and love—but the greatest of these is love." Paul's entire encouragement to love is rooted in the promise that one day we will behold God and we will know fully and be fully known.

This leads us to the next formative practice of the Christian life. As my friend has said, "The heart cannot love what the mind does not know." In order to love God, we must know God. And in order to know God, we must love Him. But there is good news: God has told us and is telling us who He is.

Reflect: Do you believe God loves you? If you believe God loves you, do you *feel* He loves you? How?

Discuss: How can our love for one another invite us deeper into reflection on the love of God?

Practice: Write down the names of five people you love. How does your love for them reflect the way God loves you?

CHAPTER 5

What Do We Know?

How happy is the one who does not
walk in the advice of the wicked
or stand in the pathway with sinners
or sit in the company of mockers!
Instead, his delight is in the LORD*'s instruction,*
and he meditates on it day and night.
He is like a tree planted beside flowing streams
that bears its fruit in its season,
and its leaf does not wither.
Whatever he does prospers.
Psalm 1:1–3

A few months back I wanted to share a song with my friend. I told him, "You have to listen to this song, it's really interesting." The song had a poppy chorus that was easy to sing and a driving beat that was fun. We sat in my living room and I played the song. About halfway through the song, as I bopped my head with the groove, my friend said, "What's this song about?" I just stared back at them blankly. I had no idea. I had probably listened to the song fifty times, but I had no idea what it was saying.

It's possible to hear without truly listening. This happens all the time in a distracted age. We hear sounds, but we aren't all there. It's easy for us to take a friend for granted when talking with them. We take a glance (or more than a glance) at our phone periodically, we start thinking about what we will say in response, our thoughts drift off to the next item on the schedule. But what would you say if I told you that God is speaking to you right now? You'd probably tell me: "There is no way I'd miss out on that!" Right? If God was speaking right now to you and me—there's no way we'd not listen to His voice!

God *is* speaking right now. And too often we are missing it. We aren't listening. Like standing next to the Grand Canyon while we play around on our phones, we live with incredible access to the revelation of God, but we settle for surface-level sounds. God is inviting us to dive deep—to hear from the living God.

One of the formative practices of the Christian life is listening to God. We turn our ears and our hearts toward the voice of the Lord and have His Word reshape our lives. Surprisingly, we are rarely told that the reason it is crucial for Christians to read and study God's Word regularly is because God's Word is not just what He spoke long ago, but the principal place He is still speaking right now. God's Word isn't just what God said; it's what God is saying. When we read and listen to God's Word, by the help and power of the Spirit, we fellowship with God. God's Word is His ongoing invitation into divine conversation—engaging our heart, soul, mind, and strength—as we listen to and speak with God through it.

You and I are invited to hear from God primarily in the Son of God Jesus Christ, in the Word of God (the Bible), and in the wonders of creation. If these don't *feel* special to us, it demonstrates our lack of understanding, not God's lack of explaining. God's Word is forming us even when it doesn't *feel* like it's doing anything. We approach listening to the voice of God with the expectations that every time we hear from God that the skies will open up, angels will descend, and trumpets will blare. But it's more ordinary. And more common. This is good news.

Let's imagine for a moment you are sitting with a five-year-old. You want to tell them you love them. What would be the clearest and kindest way you could communicate this? Sure, you could do an interpretive dance, you could recite Shakespearean poetry, you could dress up in costume and do a one-act play. But I imagine you and I both agree that if you really want the five-year-old to hear "I love you," the kindest and clearest way you could share this with them would be to simply say "I love you" and give them a hug.

In God's world, you and I are the five-year-old. We like to imagine we'd find God more believable and be more eager to listen to Him if His communication with us was full of fireworks. But the truth is: God is kind in speaking to us in fairly common ways—like words in books. We like to think we are too smart or sophisticated for something so simple, but we aren't. This is why one of the fundamental practices of Christian formation is reading, studying, listening to, and hearing from God's Word.

As we read and listen to God's Word, we hear God speaking. God's Word is shaping our lives even if we don't feel it doing anything. God's Word is "inspired" (2 Tim. 3:16); it is "living and active" (Heb. 4:12 ESV); it is "sweeter than honey" (Ps. 119:103); it is "a lamp . . . and light" (v. 105) for walking in the ways of God. God's Word is faithful instruction to walk in God's ways, but it's more than that. It's a testimony to what God has done and will do on our behalf. By the power of the Holy Spirit, God's Word *works*. I don't mean that it is practical. I mean that God's Word acts upon those who listen to it in faith. God says through the prophet Isaiah, "For just as rain and snow fall from heaven and do not return there without saturating the earth and making it germinate and sprout, and providing seed to sow and food to eat, so my word that comes from my mouth will not return to me empty, but it will accomplish what I please and will prosper in what I send it to do" (Isa. 55:10–11). We are invited to behold the God who speaks so we can become people who listen to God.

God Has Spoken, God Is Speaking

The world began with words. Not just any words, but the very words of God. The trees exist because God told them to, the waters exist because God spoke them into being, we exist because God said so. God has spoken. The signs are all around us, bearing witness to God's "eternal power and divine nature" (Rom. 1:20). God reveals His power in the wonders of the world.

This is an act of grace. God could have left the world in silence, but He didn't. God's revelation of Himself is a gift. We don't take it, we receive it. The mystery and grace are that God speaks to us at all. Why has He chosen to speak to us? Because He loves His people. God didn't just create the world with words spoken from far away; He drew near to speak to them. When we read the Genesis account of the garden, it's clear that God walked among His people, speaking to them directly. From the beginning, speaking with and hearing from God was a crucial way that humanity was intended to relate to God. It's one of the great tragedies that sin has created such disruption in our ability to hear the voice of God.

You might be thinking, *Hold on, I'm a Christian, but I don't know that I've ever heard God speaking. Where can I hear*

God? If He is speaking, I wish He would speak to me in a special way. There are certainly times when God chooses to speak in ways that are unique: He calls Moses from the burning bush (Exodus 3); He commands Isaiah's attention through a vision (Isaiah 6); He speaks through a donkey (Numbers 22); and He stuns King Belshazzar with the writing on the wall (Daniel 5). We should be quick to confess that God is free to speak in all ways that are consistent with His character and covenants, but events that showcase the unique "speech" of God should not be pitted against the normative ways we hear God in His Word, in Christ, and in the world.

God speaks to us ***in Christ Jesus***, the Son of God. Jesus Christ is the eternal "Word of God." He was in the beginning with God and He is God (John 1:1–3). Jesus Christ makes God known (John 1:18). God had spoken through the prophets, but at the right time, "he has spoken to us by his Son, whom he appointed the heir of all things, through whom also he created the world" (Heb. 1:2 ESV).

God speaks to us ***in the Bible***, His holy Word. All of Scripture, even the parts that might make us a little uncomfortable, has been "breathed out by God" (2 Tim. 3:16 ESV). The Bible is a book, but it's not like other books. It is inspired by God. It is "living and active . . . discerning the thoughts and intentions of the heart" (Heb. 4:12 ESV).

God speaks to us ***in the wonders of creation***. I once heard Jen Wilkin say, "No one stands on the edge of the Grand

Canyon and thinks, *I'm awesome.*" She's exactly right. As we look around at the natural world we are left with a distinct impression that there must be a Creator. Paul says as much in Romans 1:19–20 (ESV), "For what can be known about God is plain to them, because God has shown it to them. For his invisible attributes, namely, his eternal power and divine nature, have been clearly perceived, ever since the creation of the world, in the things that have been made. So they are without excuse." Truly, the heavens declare the glory of God.

God spoke the world into being and God is still speaking today. The only real question is: Will we listen?

Listening to God

God could have left His people in silence. Instead, He gives us the gift of His speech. All knowledge of God is grace given. Every bit of it. Becoming a person who listens to God requires a posture of reception. We don't take or earn true knowledge of who God is and what He has done, we receive it. But once God has "enlightened the eyes of our heart" (Eph. 1:18), we can practice listening to God.

In an age of distraction and entertainment, it requires discipline to listen to God. We have to "draw near to God" (James 4:8) instead of choosing lesser loves. We are tempted every day to turn our attention to the teaching that tickles our "itching ears" (2 Tim. 4:3 ESV). Because of the lingering impact of sin on our lives, we are susceptible to listening to any voice but the Lord. More than just the temptation to be led astray, when we don't lean in to listen to God, we miss an opportunity to hear His voice. Imagine I told you that tomorrow morning I was making you your favorite breakfast. I'd have it hot and ready at the table for you whenever you were ready. Am I to blame if you never come to the table and end up hungry at the end of the day? So how do we practice listening to God?

We ***sit with*** God's Word in regular Bible reading. Reading God's Word shapes us like running water over rocks. We don't often feel its impact in the moment, but over time, it shapes us bit by bit. We sit with God's Word by the routine and ordinary practice of picking up the Bible and reading. Whether you read a chapter or book of the Bible, use a Bible reading plan, listen to the Bible on your commute, regular Bible reading invites us to sit with God's Word and listen to His voice in a consistent way.

We ***sit under*** God's Word as we listen to preaching and teaching in our local churches. One of the central responsibilities of pastors is to preach God's Word to God's people. Why does God command this? Because hearing His Word preached is one of the ways we are able to listen to the voice of God. A sermon is not inspired by God the way Scripture is, but if the sermon is a faithful exposition and teaching from

God's Word, then it is one of the ways that God speaks to His people regularly through His Word.

We ***dig into*** God's Word as we study the Bible. Bible study is different from Bible reading. If Bible reading is like running water over rocks, forming us despite our ability to sense it in real time, then Bible study is like digging a well in search for the deep water. You know there is something precious buried down there, and you are willing to work a bit to get it.

We ***dwell on*** God's Word in prayer, meditation, and memorization. The psalmist says, ". . . his delight is in the LORD's instruction, and he meditates on it day and night" (Ps. 1:2). Dwelling on God's Word is moving from reading to reflection. We can do this by using God's Word as our template for our prayer (more on this in the next chapter), by meditating on God's Word (maybe writing down our reflections from the Bible in a journal), or most often by memorizing verses and passages from Scripture.

As we listen to God's Word, it will work on us; it comforts and confronts. We love the comforting, not so much the confrontation, but we need both. I have always found it interesting that Scripture is referred to as both the "breath" of God (2 Tim. 3:16 ESV) and "a two-edged sword" (Heb. 4:12 ESV). God's Word encourages us and it exhorts us. God loves us enough to speak not just what we want to hear, but also what we need to hear.

No matter how we engage with God's Word, the goal is the same: We want to see and savor God. He is the goal. His face is the prize. When we read, study, hear, or memorize the Bible, we are listening to God. God has written a book filled with His words—and He is inviting us to listen. In John 5, Jesus chastises and corrects the Jewish religious leaders because they are missing the point of God's Word. He tells them, "The Father who sent me has himself testified about me. You have not heard his voice at any time, and you haven't seen his form. You don't have his word residing in you, because you don't believe the one he sent. You pore over the Scriptures because you think you have eternal life in them, and yet they testify about me. But you are not willing to come to me so that you may have life" (vv. 37–40). People often reference this passage to suggest that God doesn't care that much if we read His Word. Of course, this isn't what Jesus is saying at all.

When Jesus corrects His audience about their Bible reading, His problem isn't with them spending too much time with God's Word. The problem is that they have the wrong goal. They are reading God's Word and missing God's face. They search the Scriptures looking for what they want to see, and in so doing, miss the fundamental thing that God's Word is intended to unveil: God.

Knowing and Encountering God

My friend J. T. loves Crossfit. He is also very particular about the dipping sauces at his favorite fast-food restaurant. I have another friend who loves pugs. She also likes flowers and teaching the Bible. They both wrote some books. So now you know a few facts about a couple of my friends. But do you *know* them? It can be a tricky question to answer. To truly know someone, we need more than just information. Certainly, we can't know someone without knowing some information about them. True knowledge is not just information but an *encounter*. Fellowship with God isn't just a perfect score on a quiz about God; it's encountering the presence of God. It's not a competition we win; it's a communion we receive.

If the goal of Christian formation is *to have our heart, mind, and strength transformed by God the Father, in Christ Jesus, through the power and presence of the Holy Spirit at work in all the ordinary affairs of our life*, then we must know God. And the good news is that God has spoken and is speaking to us. He has told us who He is. If I read God's Word, then will I know God?

The Bible is not a book like other books because God didn't just write it, He makes it come alive. The Holy Spirit who inspired the writing of God's Word, illuminates the reading of God's Word. You might say that the Holy Spirit moves us from God's pages to God's presence. He invites us to encounter God in His active Word. Augustine captured this glorious invitation when he wrote, "For now, treat the Scriptures of God as the face of God; melt in its presence."[8] The psalmist captures this truth of encountering God in His Word when he writes, "In your light do we see light" (Ps. 36:9 ESV). The Holy Spirit illuminates God's Word so that we can encounter God as we listen and read. And what do we discover when we encounter the God that Scripture reveals? The glorious face of God.

Behold/Become

Yet how many of us have started a Bible reading plan at the beginning of the year only to end up behind and ashamed by the time we reach Numbers? Most Christians have been told they *should* read God's Word, but no real reason why. We are told: It would be good to know the Bible (this is true), it's important to be reminded of truth in a world of false stories (this is true), that God's Word is good for us (also true!). But what's the real reason we should listen to God? We read because the God who created, redeemed, and is upholding the world has spoken and He is inviting you to behold Him.

We can't know God if we don't engage with His Word. Because God's Word is living and active, the knowledge we gain from it is not only information, but an encounter. We don't read the Bible merely to "grasp" God, but also to greet Him. As we meet with God in His Word, our knowledge of God increases, and so does our fellowship.

The joy of listening to God is getting to see God. As the psalmist exclaims, "I sought the LORD, and he answered me and rescued me from all my fears. Those who look to him are radiant with joy; their faces will never be ashamed. This poor man cried, and the LORD heard him and saved him from all his troubles. The angel of the LORD encamps around those who fear him, and rescues them. Taste and see that the LORD is good. How happy is the person who takes refuge in him!" (Ps. 34:4–8). As we look toward the LORD and listen to His voice, we draw near to a "radiant joy."

God's presence is the goal of reading God's Word. Many days, we will listen to God's voice and there may not be a distinct or profound sense of "radiant joy" in His presence. But those days will be like kindling, small branches and leaves piled up, just waiting for the Spirit to spark a fire. As we wait, listening to know God, we have the joy of speaking to Him in prayer. For the true God is not just the God who speaks, but also the God who hears.

Reflect: Why do you read God's Word?

Discuss: Describe a time when God's voice impacted you in a way that produced visible change.

Practice: Below are five suggestions for those who feel stuck in their engagement with God's voice:

1. *If you struggle with reading*, try listening to the Bible. Go for a walk and listen to someone read the Bible.
2. *If you struggle with memorizing Scripture*, try memorizing without the verse reference. Lots of people get hung up on "nailing the numbers." I encourage people to focus on memorizing the words of the verse and the chapter/book.
3. *If you've read the Bible (or a specific book) many times and now feel a bit bored* with the practice, try reading short books of the Bible out loud in one sitting: Ruth, Colossians, Philippians, Jude, Habakkuk.
4. *If you are someone who learns better with others*, try jumping into or starting a group Bible study.
5. *If you feel like you need a first step in Bible reading*, bring a Bible and journal to take notes during Sunday's sermon. Read the passage for the sermon ahead of Sunday service and pray this simple prayer: "Father, please speak to me through Your Word this week."

CHAPTER 6

What Has Our Attention?

"The eyes of the Lord are on the righteous
and his ears are open to their prayer."
1 Peter 3:12

A few months ago my wife and I drove halfway across Texas to see one of the most legendary rock bands in music history perform on what could be their final tour. The stadium was packed full of people. We got to our seats and found we were sitting next to a family of six. The mom and dad were as excited as we were, but ten minutes into this band's performance all four of the kids had put on their headphones and were scrolling on their phones. They were sitting in very good seats while one of the most famous bands in the history of music performed right in front of them. Lights were flashing, the music was deafening, and there were tens of thousands of people singing along. And they missed it.

I judged those kids, but honestly, I am just like them far too often. It is very difficult to pay attention to anything anymore. We have been trained by the devices of this age to give away our attention in exchange for distraction. Ten minutes of scrolling becomes two hours and all of a sudden we realize that what began by clicking on that one funny video has now sent us down a "rabbit hole."

The poet Mary Oliver said, "Attention is the beginning of devotion."[9] It's hard to be fully devoted if you are perpetually distracted. We live in an age of anxiety and entertainment. If we aren't distracting ourselves from our anxieties, we are simply too anxious to be entertained. We use our phones, social media, and streaming as both pacifier and catalyst. When we are stressed, we check out into a digital desert that promises us an oasis that is always an illusion. We might feel satisfied for a moment, but we walk away empty. What has our attention will have our acts. What captures our presence will become the place we pin our prayers.

We know that we need more than distraction. We are desperate to be seen. We are longing to be heard. Like Israel crying out in Egypt, our burdens are great and we need help. It's often easier to settle for shadows over substance, but what would happen if we came to believe that God listens to His people? That at any moment of the day, anywhere, we have God's undivided attention. Prayer is the fundamental act of giving God our devoted attention. Prayer is really attentiveness to the presence of God; the God who speaks and the God who hears. God's people are invited to behold this God—to give Him our attention as we fellowship with Him—so that we can become people who speak with God.

God Is Listening

We may not be paying attention to God, but He is paying attention to us. It's not a chore for Him. He is not stressed out by our need. When we cry out to God, it never goes to voicemail. He doesn't leave us on "read." God hears His people. God created us for fellowship with Him. He isn't bothered by it; He delights in it.

It's not just that God is listening; He is *inviting* us to speak to Him: "In the morning, LORD, you hear my voice; in the morning I plead my case to you and watch expectantly" (Ps. 5:3). The Lord is eager to hear from the citizens of His kingdom. Immediately after Jesus teaches His followers the Lord's Prayer, He commends a "shameless boldness" (Luke 11:8) to be persistent in prayer. God isn't overhearing us accidentally; He is listening on purpose.

But if God knows all things, why would He need to listen? He doesn't *need* to listen. He *wants* to listen. When we cry out to God in prayer, we aren't sharing new information with God. He is never surprised by what we speak to Him.

He invites our prayers not because He lacks information, but because He loves His children.

I love the sound of my daughter's voice. Even if I already know what she is going to say, I love to hear her say it. In a similar way, I know my father loves me, but when he looks me in the eye and says, "I love you, son," I can feel my heart swell. I already *knew* the information, but I delight in hearing it again. God isn't listening to learn; He is listening with love.

How can we speak to God? We have been given access to the "house of God" (Heb. 10:21) through the "blood of Jesus" (Heb. 10:19). We are invited to "ask, seek, and knock" (Luke 5) on the King's door in the middle of the night. Tim Keller said it best, "The only person who dares wake up a king at 3:00 a.m. for a glass of water is a child. We have that kind of access."[10] We can speak to God because He is willing to hear us.

Though, if we are honest, it can sometimes feel as if God isn't hearing our prayers. The same psalmist who rejoices that God "watches expectantly" as he prays in the morning will cry out (more than once), "How long, Lord? Will you forget me forever? How long will you hide your face from me? How long will I store up anxious concerns within me, agony in my mind every day?" (Ps. 13:1–2). The truth is: sometimes it *feels* like prayer is pointless.

What do we do when we feel as if God isn't listening? We listen to God. We open up God's Word and we anchor ourselves in the truth of His voice. If you hike up a winding trail and get lost, what do you do? Do you assume that there is no longer any true north? Do you resign yourself to wandering aimlessly forever? Of course not. You pull out your map and your compass and you reorient yourself. You don't discover what's true by looking deeper inside of your confusion; you look at something that is clear, true, and outside of yourself.

God is listening to His people. Not because He needs to, but because He wants to hear the voice of His children. Even when we don't feel like God hears us, "the eyes of the Lord are on the righteous and his ears are open to their prayer" (1 Pet. 3:12). God hears His people. His attention is on you, even when yours is far from Him. Always and forever.

We Are Listening

Have you ever tried to have a private conversation somewhere really loud? Maybe you were at a football game, or a concert, or a lively party. The music is humming, the space is filled with the noise of movement, other people are talking or yelling. It may be so loud that you turn to the person next to you and you can see them speaking, but you can't hear what they are saying. You have to lean in closer. Sometimes you have to put your ear right up next to their mouth. Or maybe you have been at the other end of a field from someone trying to tell you something. You can hear the faint sounds of their voice, but you can't make out what they are saying. You can tell they are trying to speak to you, but you can't hear them. What do you do? You get closer to them.

Our worlds are full of noise. And we are listening. What we consume shapes us. We end up living in light of what we listen to because what has our attention will take our devotion and whatever has our devotion will direct our worship.

When we discover God is listening to His people, our immediate response is to think we should start talking more. This is why our prayers often are so light on praise and so heavy on petition. Engaging in prayer begins with beholding God. This is how Jesus teaches us to pray in the Lord's Prayer. Where do we begin when we approach God in prayer? "Our Father in heaven, your name be honored as holy. Your kingdom come. Your will be done on earth as it is in heaven" (Matt. 6:9–10).

Our prayer will be strengthened when we begin with listening. In the midst of our noisy lives, we begin prayer by pausing, by waiting, by entering silently so that we can be reminded that we are approaching the holy God. One moment Moses is tending sheep in the hills, then all of a sudden he is called into the presence of God. As Moses nears the burning bush, we discover the tension of speaking to God in prayer: He calls Moses by name and tells him to remove his sandals because he is on holy ground. This is God's invitation to His people: draw near to My presence for I know you, but realize whose presence you are in.

To pray is to listen to God. Not just to listen to His words in Scripture, but to enter into an awareness of His presence. The psalmist reflects us on this dynamic in Psalm 131:1–3: "LORD, my heart is not proud; my eyes are not haughty. I do not get involved with things too great or too wondrous for me. Instead, I have calmed and quieted my soul like a weaned child with its mother; my soul is like a weaned child. Israel, put your hope in the LORD, both now and forever."

As we pray, we will speak with God. We will confess to Him, we will praise Him, we will make requests, we will give thanks to Him. But in order to speak to God, we will need to regularly turn our attention away from the noise of the world around us so we can listen for the voice of God.

We Can Speak to God

I am not interested in your pet. Not even a little bit. If you start talking to me about something funny your dog did last night, I will politely nod along. I will smirk as you tell me that they did something so silly because they are such a cutesy pie. I might even chuckle. But you should know, I am being polite. While you talk, I am thinking about something else. You don't have my full attention. Am I a monster? I don't think so. I'm just not that interested in animals. (If you are a pet lover and need to put the book down to take a breath and pray for me, please do so now.)

You may love hearing about other people's pets, but I am sure there is something you will not pay attention to. You and I have limits. We have limits on what we are interested in, limits on our attention, limits on our knowledge, limits on our power, limits on our time. We have all sorts of constraints on our capacity. This is part of being a creature. We are limited. These limitations aren't a result of sin, they are created limitations.

But God has none of these limitations. We can speak to Him about anything, from anywhere, at any time. We don't have to catch him up, He doesn't need time to "think about it," His schedule is never too full, He never gets confused, and He never gets distracted. Our attention may be shrinking every year, but God's attention never slacks. Never.

So what will we say to God? Two pitfalls keep people from active prayer: either they don't know what to say or they don't know how to say it. If we wait until we are perfect at praying, we will never start. Eugene Peterson, in his book on prayer, *Answering God*, captures God's invitation to speak to him so wonderfully: "Prayer is primal speech. We do not first learn how to do it, and then proceed to do it; we do it, in the doing we find out what we are doing, and then deepen and mature in it."[11]

Sometimes I feel like I am just praying the same old things over and over again. But years ago, Donald Whitney helped me discover one of the simplest and most fruitful ways to pray: praying the Bible.[12] We speak back to God in prayer what He has already spoken to us. We use God's Word to structure our prayers. Yes, we can use the format of the Lord's Prayer. Absolutely! But we don't have to stop there: we can pray through the Psalms, the Prophets, and the Gospels. All of God's Word can function as a way of formatting our prayer life. When we use God's Word as our foundation, we don't have to think of what to say; we don't have to be creative. We can simply read God's Word and then allow it to lead us in the right direction for prayer.

But how do we pray? We pray to God the Father through God the Son by the power of God the Holy Spirit. And we can use our normal language. We don't have to be artistic with our prayers. Sometimes my prayers sound serious, sometimes they sound silly. Sometimes I burp when I pray, but hopefully not at the dinner table or around others. Other times I pray when I go to the bathroom. I pray while driving. (Don't worry, I keep my eyes open for those prayer sessions.)

If we are going to learn to "pray without ceasing" (1 Thess. 5:17 ESV), then it will require us to dramatically lower our expectations of fanciful and glittering prayer lives. We will have to be prepared to pray rough-and-ready prayers that will sometimes feel more like cries and shouts for help than hymns of praise. But we can take heart knowing that even when we are weak and don't know "what to pray for as we should . . . the Spirit himself intercedes for us with inexpressible groanings" (Rom. 8:26). What a marvelous grace! The God who hears the prayers of His people is the God who helps His people pray.

Practicing Prayer

Now we're talking about practice. Not a game, but practice. In the journey of *having our heart, mind, and strength transformed by God,* we engage in "formative practices." How can we become people who speak with and hear from God? We practice prayer. Because so many feel like their prayer life is paralyzed, I want to provide seven biblical and basic ways to ignite your prayer life. Remember, God hears His people anytime, anywhere, about anything. As the psalmist reminds us in Psalm 139, "Where can I go to escape your Spirit? Where can I flee from your presence? If I go up to heaven, you are there; if I make my bed in Sheol, you are there" (vv. 7–8). These tips won't make God more able to hear you, but they might make you more consistent in faithful and fruitful prayer.

Pray Scripture.

Whether you use the Lord's Prayer, the Psalms, or another passage of Scripture, use God's Word to structure and shape your prayers. God's Word is inspired by God for "teaching, for rebuking, for correcting, for training in righteousness, so that the man of God may be complete, equipped for every good work" (2 Tim. 3:16–17). God uses His Word to "judge the thoughts and intentions of the heart" (Heb. 4:12). Using God's Word as the template and platform for our prayer will provide direction and help for our practice.

Seek silence.

In a world full of noise, pursue silence. Prayer is speaking with and listening to God. To listen fully requires your attention; to speak meaningfully requires your attention. In Luke 5 we hear that Jesus would often withdraw to desolate places to pray. Why? Jesus knew the value of silence and solitude. He wanted to give His full attention to God the Father in the prayer of fellowship. Get up early. Go for a walk. Hide from your kids in the bathroom and leave your phone in the kitchen. Even if you can only get silence and solitude for a moment, find it. Get to a quiet place and say: "Lord Jesus, have mercy on me. Help me. Speak to me."

Practice Sabbath.

The law of Moses has been fulfilled in Christ Jesus. We don't have to treat the law as a tyrant that demands too much, but we can listen to the law as a tutor in the ways of righteousness. God's people are invited to rest with God. The Sabbath is provided as a weekly opportunity to cease from work in order to give attention to God. Sabbath is intended to be a day of faith and trust that we enter into prayerfully. It's a day where we can pray to the Lord: "God, I'm not holding this whole thing together. You are."

Consider fasting.

Jesus assumes that we will occasionally fast for the purposes of focused prayer. Right after He instructs His followers in the Lord's Prayer, He tells them, "Whenever you fast" (Matt. 6:16). He gives them instructions on how to fast in a way that honors the Lord. Fasting is deliberately abstaining from something(s) for a spiritual purpose, specifically, for the purpose of focused and desperate prayer.

Pray with others.

Ask any pastor what the most poorly attended event in their church is and they will tell you it's the prayer meeting.

I heard an old pastor once tell a group of us young ministry leaders, "If you want people to come to your prayer meeting, just tell them it's a business meeting." It's sad, but true. Praying with others is one of the best ways to deepen your prayer life. We shouldn't be too surprised, when we hear about the church that is birthed at Pentecost, one of the key markers of their life together was devoting "themselves to the apostles' teaching, to the fellowship, to the breaking of bread, and to prayer" (Acts 2:42).

Pray on the spot.

Praying for others is called intercession. We are regularly encouraged in Scripture to pray for other people (1 Tim. 2:1–2; Eph. 6:18). I find that when someone asks for prayer, it's easy for me to say, "Yes, I will pray for you," and I mean it when I say it. But then I walk off to the next thing and forget. Maybe you do this too? Let me encourage you: Pray upon request. If someone asks you at church, "Would you keep me in your prayers this week?" Pause right then and there and say: "Let's pray now." We worship the God who hears our prayers—there is no reason to delay for a better time. We can speak with God here and now.

Ask for prayer.

We all need prayer. One of the ways we can become people who speak with God is by asking others to pray for us. Like the apostle Paul asks the church in Thessalonica, "Brothers and sisters, pray for us that the word of the Lord may spread rapidly and be honored, just as it was with you, and that we may be delivered from wicked and evil people, for not all have faith" (2 Thess. 3:1–2). When we ask for prayer from others, we receive the opportunity to listen in on a conversation with God and to remember that God doesn't just hear our prayers, but He hears the prayers of all of His people.

Behold/Become

Jesus never stops interceding on behalf of His people. God hears His people because Christ has saved us a seat and speaks on our behalf. It is through Jesus Christ and the power of the Holy Spirit that our prayers are brought into the presence of God. In Hebrews 7 we are told, "He is able to save completely those who come to God through him, since he always lives to intercede for them" (v. 25). If this isn't enough, we hear the same thing in Romans 8, "Who is the one who condemns? Christ Jesus is the one who died, but even more, has been raised; he also is at the right hand of God and intercedes for us" (v. 34).

Consider the glory of this: When you stop praying, Christ doesn't. When you say "Amen" and go on to the next thing, Christ is still at the right hand of God the Father interceding on your behalf. It's because Christ's intercession is unending that the Father hears our prayers at all. Our prayer is brought into God's presence in Christ by the power of the Holy Spirit. God is inviting us to give our attention to Him. Not as one thing in a long list of priorities, but as the center of our attention, the anchor of our devotion. He knows we are longing to be seen and heard. He knows the full extent of our neediness, and He is inviting us to walk into the courts of the King of kings anytime and have His ear about anything.

Prayer is the beginning of praise. We are led to rejoicing as we reflect upon the God who hears. When we give God our attention in prayer, we are invited into the courts of the Lord, where we behold that the God who hears is also the God who rejoices.

Reflect: Have you ever felt as if God didn't hear your prayers? Why did it feel that way?

Discuss: Is there a time where you (or your church) saw God answer specific prayers in a powerful way?

Practice: Below are four practices to encourage and deepen your prayer life:

1. Pray before your Bible reading/study: One of the key ways we hear from God is through His Word. Take time before you read, study, or listen to the Bible to thank God for speaking and ask Him to illuminate His Word.
2. Pray the Psalms: Praying the Psalms regularly has been the most significant and formative prayer practice of my life with God. Start with Psalm 1 and work your way through all 150 psalms.
3. Postured prayer: Change the way you position your body as you pray. Pray kneeling, pray face down, pray walking, pray sitting with palms up and open, or pray with your hands covering your face. Allow your posture to reflect the content of your prayers.
4. Practice Sabbath: If you are uncomfortable with silence and solitude, take a journal, your Bible (not on your device), a pen, and go somewhere you can be alone and quiet for two hours. Read God's Word, pray, and stay off of your digital devices.

CHAPTER 7

What Do We Worship?

"Do not fear; Zion, do not let your hands grow weak. The Lord *your God is among you, a warrior who saves. He will rejoice over you with gladness. He will be quiet in his love. He will delight in you with singing."*
Zephaniah 3:16–17

There's a beautiful picture in *The Magician's Nephew* from C. S. Lewis's Chronicles of Narnia series. Narnia is not built brick-by-brick or by painstakingly following a blueprint. Instead, Narnia is created in song: "The Voice on the earth was now louder and more triumphant. . . . The Voice rose and rose, till all the air was shaking with it. And just as it swelled to the mightiest and most glorious sound it had yet produced, the sun arose. . . . They made you feel excited; until you saw the Singer himself, and then you forgot everything else."[13] The creation of Narnia reflects the creation of our world.

The world begins with the overflow of worship, delight, and rejoicing, and not our own: it is the voice of God Himself that rings out. God is not worshipping creation but is delighting in His fellowship within Himself as Father, Son, and Spirit, moved to speak out of that delight. In order to grasp this picture, it may help to think of a chocolate fountain. Stick with me for a moment.

I can still remember the first time I saw one. I was stunned. It was a marvel of engineering. I couldn't believe everyone at the wedding reception wasn't just standing around the table looking at it. Liquid chocolate cascading down silver discs. Ready for dipping marshmallows, strawberries, maybe some angel food cake. I was a ten-year-old boy and it was one of the most amazing things I had seen up to that point in my life. Admittedly: I hadn't seen much.

The fountain had chocolate spouting from the top, trickling down to the bottom like sheets of sweetness, only to then be recycled up to the top to begin its delicious journey all over again. It is an endless loop of delectable delight. Every time I see a fountain (even a chocolate one), I can't help but to think of God. It doesn't surprise me that fountains have historically been used as images or symbols of the divine, even among Christian theologians and writers.

The one true God of the world, the God of the Bible, is Trinity: God eternally exists as one essence in three distinct persons, each of whom is fully God, and yet there is one

God. In simpler terms: God is three in one. God eternally exists in an unbroken, unchanging, delighting fellowship of Father, Son, and Holy Spirit. When God creates the world, He doesn't create out of a lack or need, but out of the deliberate overflow of trinitarian abundance. In this way, creation occurs as a result of rejoicing.

Throughout the story of the Bible we discover that God rejoices. God rejoices in God and God rejoices over His people. Consider the words of the prophet Zephaniah who says,

> Sing for joy, Daughter Zion; shout loudly, Israel! Be glad and celebrate with all your heart, Daughter Jerusalem! The LORD has removed your punishment; he has turned back your enemy. The King of Israel, the LORD, is among you; you need no longer fear harm. On that day it will be said to Jerusalem: "Do not fear; Zion, do not let your hands grow weak. The LORD your God is among you, a warrior who saves. He will rejoice over you with gladness. He will be quiet in his love. He will delight in you with singing." (Zeph. 3:14–17)

Why should the people rejoice and celebrate? Because God has brought salvation, but more than that, He "rejoices over you with gladness . . . delights in you with singing." God rejoices in you like a father rejoices in the first steps of his child.

We often think of worship as that which is "owed" to God. In this way of thinking, worship is what we "ought" to do because God is worthy of it. This is true—God is worthy of our worship and we ought to worship God. But this isn't the only thing true of our worship. It's also true that our worship is meant to be the return of rejoicing. In worship, we are welcomed into God's eternal fellowship of rejoicing, it's like a chorus sung together, not a solo. Our worship is a response to the delight of God that billows over into all the world. When we behold the God who rejoices over His people, we become people who rejoice in God.

God Is Glorious

Don't tell anyone, but I had a bit of a glorious high school soccer career. I was a goalie, because who wants to do all of that running? I won some awards, collected some trophies, and got my name in the local paper. But that's where it stopped. I was a big fish in a small pond, and while I was good in our little slice of the world, it's a really big world and I wasn't that good. A few years back, as I was helping my parents move from my childhood house to a new place, we found a moldy box in the back of the garage. We opened it up and discovered all of my old trophies, but they had lost their shine. They were dusty, filthy, and crumbling. Their gold plates were gone, replaced with rust. There is only one glory that doesn't fade—we can receive it, but it doesn't belong to us by nature.

God is glorious. We say this all the time in churches. We talk about God's glory and the glory of God. But I find that most have no real idea what it means to say that God is glorious. Here is a simple way to think about it: God's glory is the shining forth of God's perfection, power, and presence. God's glory shines like the sun, lighting up all other things with its own light. God's glory is the spotlight of His splendor.

We don't have to imagine that this is the case. God tells us that when the world is finally made right, fully made new, we won't even need the sun or lamps any longer because the Lord God will be our light. The glory of the eternal God is not just the source of light at the end of the story, it's the source of life at the beginning of the story.

Creation is sung out by the very words of God. Why do the "heavens declare the glory of God" (Ps. 19:1)? Because they were "made by the word of the Lord, and all the stars, by the breath of his mouth" (Ps. 33:6). We are to "Rejoice in the Lord . . . praise the Lord . . . sing a new song to him . . . for the word of the Lord is right . . . the earth is full of the Lord's unfailing love" (Ps. 33:1–5). God delights in His world. God delights in His people. God loves His church. God rejoicing in His own splendor, the delighting love of the Father, Son, and Holy Spirit, is the grounds for our worship.

All of our rejoicing is rooted in the rejoicing of God. Even when it is misdirected toward the glory of creaturely things, the problem isn't our desire to worship, it's the direction of it. This is the tragedy Paul speaks of in Romans 1:

> For though they knew God, they did not glorify him as God or show gratitude. Instead, their thinking became worthless, and their senseless hearts were darkened. Claiming to be wise, they became fools and exchanged the glory of the immortal God for images resembling mortal man, birds, four-footed animals, and reptiles. Therefore God delivered them over in the desires of their hearts to sexual impurity, so that their bodies were degraded among themselves. They exchanged the truth of God for a lie, and worshiped and served what has been created instead of the Creator, who is praised forever. Amen. (vv. 21–25)

We are designed to worship. The problem isn't *that* we worship, but *what* we worship.

What happens when our worship is given to the wrong things? We become debased. Our idolatry diminishes us. When we rejoice in God, we become what God has already declared us to be. When we worship what God has created, we become less than what God has designed us to be. We are worshippers. It's unavoidable. The only question is: What (or who) will we worship?

We Are Worshippers

Worship is natural for us. Worshipping God is not natural for us. We are naughty by nature, so our worship is broken from the beginning. But don't be confused: You and I *are* worshippers. When we "taste and see" something we like, we celebrate it. We proclaim it to others. We rejoice in whatever we relish. How many times has someone told you: "You've got to go see this movie!" "You really must try that new restaurant that just opened up!" "You have to hear this song!"

We are worshippers by nature, but our worship is misdirected. This is why the Bible has so much to say about idols and idolatry. An idol is anyone or anything that receives the attention, affection, and allegiance that should be given to God. Idolatry is the act of giving those things away to something or someone other than God. Idols are captivating, not just because we are susceptible to temptation, but also because we are designed to worship. When we fall into sin, we aren't just indulging an idol, we are giving our worship away. As we've already established, we become what we behold. When we worship idols, they transform us into their image.

In Exodus 32 we find a strange and heartbreaking tale of Israel's idolatry after God delivered them from Egypt. God had allowed Israel to plunder the Egyptians on their way out of town, taking gold from the very people who had kept them in chains for centuries. But when their deliverance is delayed at Mt. Sinai, the people cry out for a god to worship. So Aaron melted down their gold and made the calf. God speaks to Moses on the mountain to warn him about Israel's transgression, but listen to what He says:

> The LORD spoke to Moses: "Go down at once! For your people you brought up from the land of Egypt have acted corruptly. . . . they have made for themselves an image of a calf. They have bowed down to it, sacrificed to it, and said, "Israel, these are your gods, who brought you up from the land of Egypt." The LORD also said to Moses, "I have seen this people, and they are indeed a stiff-necked people." (vv. 7–9)

The Lord tells Moses of Israel's idolatry in making the calf. Then He refers to Israel as a "stiff-necked" people. This phrase, "stiff-necked," refers to a beast of burden—an animal like an ox or donkey. What has Israel become in their worship of the golden calf? They became what they beheld. This didn't just happen back then; it happens to us now. Sin always curves us in upon ourselves, making us less than we were created to be. Think about Mr. Scrooge from the classic

Charles Dickens tale. His greed and selfishness had basically twisted and knotted him up into a man who was embittered, unhappy, and hateful. People who idolize control end up consumed with anger at the least inconvenience; people who idolize comfort end up crippled with fear at the prospect of risk; and people who make idols out of satisfaction end up losing their lives to the never-ending lust for more.

We find this logic throughout the story of Scripture. Consider Psalm 115, "Their idols are silver and gold, made by human hands. They have mouths but cannot speak, eyes, but cannot see. They have ears but cannot hear, noses, but cannot smell. They have hands but cannot feel, feet, but cannot walk. They cannot make a sound with their throats. Those who make them are just like them, as are all who trust in them" (vv. 4–8). As G. K. Beale has said so wonderfully, "What people revere, they resemble, either for ruin or restoration."[14]

Don't think about worship as the mere singing of songs. Certainly, worship can overflow into song and Christian worship is cultivated and expressed in part by singing, but when I say that we are worshippers by nature, I mean we are creatures of desire and delight. We are always looking for a fitting home for our allegiance, affection, and assent. What is true worship? "To present your bodies as a living sacrifice, holy and pleasing to God; this is your true worship. Do not be conformed to this age, but be transformed by the renewing of your mind, so that you may discern what is the good, pleasing, and perfect will of God" (Rom. 12:1–2).

When we give our worship away to idols, we become ruined. When we direct our worship toward God, we become restored. Our worship, both individually and corporately, is central to *the journey of having our heart, mind, and strength transformed by God the Father, in Christ Jesus, through the power and presence of the Holy Spirit.* We are not designed for ruin but for restoration, found in fellowship with God.

How Do We Worship?

The practice of worship involves more than just our words. Our worship is a whole life practice, encompassing all the ordinary affairs of life, even including eating and drinking (1 Cor. 10:31). In God's world, for God's people, every act is an opportunity for worship. Our jobs, our hobbies, our workouts, our friendships, our parties, our funerals, our dating, our marriage, our parenting, our victories, and our failures; everything is an opportunity to proclaim with the apostle Paul, "For from him and through him and to him are all things. To him be the glory forever. Amen" (Rom. 11:36). We should be worship generalists, looking at every action, thought, and conversation as an opportunity to bear witness and praise to God.

Paul captures the heart of the worship generalist in Colossians 3, "Whatever you do, do it from the heart, as something done for the Lord and not for people, knowing that you will receive the reward of an inheritance from the Lord. You serve the Lord Christ" (vv. 23–24). We are worshipping at all times. Every moment is an offering, rendered either to the true God or to something else.

We see this whole life dimension of worship when we look at Israel at Sinai. As God has delivered them from Egypt, He gives them detailed direction on how they are to now live in His presence. God's presence in their midst means that everything must be reoriented to life in His presence. We often read the laws about washing, eating, drinking, altars, Sabbath days, where you can go and when and we think to ourselves: *Why does God care about all these small matters?* But the more we come to see the holy glory of God, the more we are left thinking that the Old Testament laws aren't too detailed, they may not be specific enough! To see the glory of God is to see His power and His holiness—a holiness He has invited us to join Him in, which feels like a tall order, and we might just need a little more guidance. We need God's help to live in the presence of God's holiness.

Imagine for a moment that you and I are sitting in your living room after dinner. As we sit there, a little puppy walks into the room. It's not your puppy, it's not mine. Neither of us know where it came from. Our behaviors would adjust a little bit. We might shift how we are sitting, we begin to ask some questions, we might be a little nervous given that an unknown animal has just entered the room. But it's a puppy—we aren't too alarmed. Now imagine the same scene, but this time a lion walks into the room. It's not your lion, it's not mine. Neither of us know where it came from. Do we react differently from when we met the puppy? Absolutely. But why, the lion and the puppy are both animals and they are both unknown to us. The answer is obvious: there is a difference in power.

When the Lord takes up residence in the midst of the people of rescued Israel, a Lion has entered the room. Everything now changes for Israel. They are in the presence of God's glory. His holy power is at the center of their lives. When we realize that we live in the very presence of God, we come to realize that worship requires our whole lives.

Where Do We Worship?

If worship involves all of life, then where do we begin? Like standing in front of a buffet, if our plate can be filled with anything and everything, it can be hard to know where to start. We don't want to minimize the scope of worship, but we do want to have clarity on how to walk in worship. Are there rules for rejoicing? Well, yeah, sort of.

I want to point you toward four domains of worship: personal worship, corporate worship, household worship, and public worship.

1. Personal worship is marked by the formative practices we are exploring in this book: prayer, reading Scripture, obedience, love, hope, spiritual battle. When we engage in these formative practices, we are offering worship unto the Lord.

2. Corporate worship is the weekly gathering of God's people to remember and rehearse the mighty acts of God as we fellowship in His presence. Our corporate worship is shaped by practices and rites that are unique to that domain, specifically: baptism and the Lord's Supper. When we gather as God's people, we sit under the preached Word of God, we pray together, we fellowship with one another, we baptize people into the family of God, and we feast at the Lord's Table together.

Over the last few years, due to both hurdles and temptations, many have decided that in-person weekly worship is either optional or hindered by obstacles. It's worth reminding ourselves that one of the central reasons God calls His people to regularly gather in worship with one another is so that we may provoke one another toward "love and good works" (Heb. 10:24). Gathering with God's people in corporate worship is the ground level for our spiritual formation. You can build on top of it, but if you try to build a life formed by Christ without it, you will find anything you build ends up wobbly.

3. Household worship is the opportunity we have to bring the story of God right into the center of our homes. All throughout Israel's story, God tells His people to speak the story of His redemption to the next generation, just as Israel built altars, established Ebenezers, and ate meals to remember and rehearse the story. Household worship is a crucial way that we engage in the journey of formation together. Household worship is the way we embody the words of Joshua, "But if it doesn't please you to worship the LORD, choose for yourselves today: Which will you worship—the gods your ancestors worshiped beyond the Euphrates River or the gods of the Amorites in whose land you are living? As for me and my family, we will worship the LORD" (Josh. 24:15).

4. Our public worship is practiced as we proclaim God's good news to the world around us. Bearing witness in this way is often called mission, which is an acceptable way to think of public worship, but what is mission? We join in the mission of God when we declare His wondrous works to the world. As many have pointed out before, mission is the practice of public worship. When we share the good news of the gospel, when we engage in intercessory prayer, when we defy the false gods of this age and culture by engaging in mercy and justice, we proclaim and perform the kingdom of God to a watching world.

The journey of Christian formation involves a holistic approach to worship. Our rejoicing is rooted in the rejoicing of God. From the very beginning, we were meant to reflect the glory of God to the world. We were designed to live in God's delighting presence and to welcome the world into the joy of its fellowship. This isn't just what the world was designed to be, it's where the world is headed.

Behold/Become

Our worship is rooted in the rejoicing God. We celebrate because He celebrates. God rejoices over His people, so we rejoice in God. I have heard Him called "the singing God," calling our attention back to Zephaniah's words: "Sing for joy, Daughter Zion; shout loudly, Israel! Be glad and celebrate with all your heart, Daughter Jerusalem! The LORD has removed your punishment. . . . He will rejoice over you with gladness. He will be quiet in his love. He will delight in you with singing" (Zeph. 3:14–17).

God doesn't worship us. I can't have you misunderstand me on this point. God rejoices in His people because His people exist as the purposeful overflow of His own delighting love in and of Himself. As image-bearers of God, we exist because of God's eternal delight in Himself. And at the end of the story, we find ourselves beholding God, rejoicing. The future heaven that will last forever needs no temple for worship. "I did not see a temple in it, because the Lord God the Almighty and the Lamb are its temple. The city does not need the sun or the moon to shine on it, because the glory of God illuminates it, and its lamp is the Lamb. . . . They will bring the glory and honor of the nations into it. Nothing unclean will ever enter it, nor anyone who does what is detestable or false, but only those written in the Lamb's book of life" (Rev. 21:22–27).

God's people will rejoice in God forever. As they see His face, His name will be printed on their foreheads (Rev. 22:4). Created to reflect Him and to fellowship with Him, we will find ourselves at the end of the story, visibly marked by Him. Our rejoicing imprinted upon us. Our worship written forever upon us. Marked by His magnificence.

Reflect: What are the most tempting idols in your life? How does it impact you when you give your worship to them?

Discuss: When you hear the word *worship*, what's the first practice that comes to mind?

Practice: What's one way you could turn toward rejoicing in God during the following events:

- Breakfast, lunch, and dinner
- Birthday parties
- Saturdays
- Visits to the hospital/urgent care clinic
- Commuting to and from work

CHAPTER 8

What Are Our Habits?

Pursue peace with everyone, and holiness—
without it no one will see the Lord.
Hebrews 12:14

I married a rule follower. It doesn't matter whether the rule seems silly or serious, my wife is going to keep it. It's not like I'm some kind of rule-breaking bad boy, but every once in a while I might use an "Employee Only" bathroom if it's the only thing available. When you got to go, you got to go.

We are all born rule breakers, but rules are good. There are better and worse ways to behave in God's world. We aren't supposed to be living however we want. There is a way that the world is designed to work. It was created with order, structure, and it was designed to be good. But pretty early on, we all broke one rule. The first domino to fall wasn't just the wrong fruit from the wrong tree, it was an act of spiritual rebellion against God. We had untainted fellowship with God and others but wanted an empire of our own. We looked at God's kingdom and imagined we could do better. We were terribly wrong.

As we've already established, we are born beholders. But our vision is broken and misdirected. We have a broken compass. We have homeless hearts. Because of this, our habits, behavior, and actions are unrighteous. As some have said, we are born unable and unwilling to do what is right in God's eyes. Like Paul writes in Romans 3, "There is no one righteous, not even one. There is no one who understands; there is no one who seeks God. . . . There is no one who does what is good, not even one" (vv. 10–12).

But we weren't created to live broken lives of unrighteous and unholy practice: "For we are his workmanship, created in Christ Jesus for good works, which God prepared ahead of time for us to do" (Eph. 2:10). We were created by God to walk in the ways of God. We were created to be righteous, to be holy. The apostle Peter says this very thing, when he quotes from Leviticus in 1 Peter 1, "As obedient children, do not be conformed to the desires of your former ignorance. But as the one who called you is holy, you also are to be holy in all your conduct; for it is written, 'Be holy, because I am holy'" (vv. 14–16).

The journey to become a holy person is really the adventure of becoming what God has already declared us to be in Christ Jesus. This journey involves habits and practices of obedience to God's will and God's Word, but it *begins* by beholding. When we behold the holiness of God, we can become people marked by holiness.

God Is Holy

I get frustrated by magic tricks. I'm the problem, not the magician. He's there to entertain, but my desire to know exactly how it works will ruin my ability to enjoy the illusion. What is intended as entertainment becomes anxiety. The magician must keep the "power" hidden, to unveil it would be to ruin the whole experience, but I want it out in the open. I want to examine it.

The holiness of God is not hidden. It is out in the open and it can be examined, but it is not an illusion from the hand of a grand magician. From the very beginning of Scripture, we are confronted by the reality: God is holy. Why does humanity's rebellion merit judgment? Because God is holy. When the divine name is revealed to Moses in Exodus 3, what does Yahweh tell Moses as he approaches the burning bush? "'Do not come closer,' [God] said. 'Remove the sandals from your feet, for the place where you are standing is holy ground'" (v. 5). When the prophet Isaiah is brought in a vision into the throne room of God, what does he encounter? Angels circling around the Lord's throne calling out to one another, "Holy, holy, holy is the Lord of Armies; his glory fills the whole earth" (Isa. 6:3). You know how you can tell when something is important in Scripture? When it's repeated three times. For perspective, this only happens one time, with one attribute of God. God's Word tells us over and over again: God is holy.

But what is holiness? When we say God is holy, we mean to say that *God is utterly unique in His perfections, purity, power, and presence.* There is nothing and no one who can compare with God. To use a big fancy word: God is *transcendent.* He is beyond any created thing. He is set apart. What happens when Moses encounters God's holiness? He hides his face. What happens when Isaiah encounters the holy God? He cries out, "Woe is me for I am ruined" (Isa. 6:5). God's holiness confronts the unrighteousness of humanity and the brokenness of the world. If we want fellowship with God, we must be holy. And in order to become holy, we must first come to see that we are wicked.

Like the X-ray at the doctor's office, we don't always want to see what might be wrong. We know something isn't as it should be, but we are a bit scared to look. God's holiness exposes our wickedness. It shows us what is out of alignment with God's will and design. It points out the problems. But it doesn't just identify the problem, it provides the solution. After Moses hides his face at the burning bush, God tells him: "I have come down to rescue [my people]. . . . I will certainly be with you" (Exod. 3:8, 12). After Isaiah cries out in anguish, what happens next? We are told that an angel brings a burning coal from the altar of the Lord, touches Isaiah's mouth with it and pronounces, "Now that this has touched your lips, your iniquity is removed and your sin is atoned for" (Isa. 6:7).

The God who is holy, is the God who is love, is the God who is gracious. He is God. Utterly unique, transcendent, set apart, and the only God who can make unholy things holy. This God who rescues His people, forgives their sins, and atones for their sin is the same God who will commission and call them to obey His holy commands. He declares us holy so that we can then become holy.

We Can Be Holy

I don't watch cartoons. I'm not trying to act like I'm too mature for cartoons (I already confessed my love for professional wrestling). I just have never connected with cartoons. But a while back a friend sent me a clip from a cartoon I've never watched, and the scene was so powerful that I just couldn't get it out of my head. At one point in the clip, the main character begins to panic and asks, "Do you, do you think it's too late for me? Am I just doomed to be the person that I am? It's not too late for me, it's not too late . . . I need you to tell me that it's not too late. I need you to tell me that it's not too late. I need you to tell me that I'm a good person. I know that I can be selfish, and narcissistic, and self-destructive, but underneath all that, deep down, I'm a good person and I need you to tell me that I'm good . . . Please, tell me that I'm good."[15]

You might be thinking: *Boy, they sure seem to be making serious cartoons these days.* You aren't wrong. In that scene, the character's selfishness, arrogance, and bad behavior has been publicly uncovered. He is shaken by the realization that he has catastrophically failed. He's left pleading for the possibility that he still has time to become good.

As we discovered above, God's holiness exposes and confronts us. But God doesn't leave us flailing in our filth, He covers us. There are real consequences to disobedience under God's holy judgment, but He always provides the covering we need. Before Adam and Eve are exiled from the garden for rebelling against God, God promises them a coming salvation and covers their shameful nakedness (Gen. 3:21).

We are called to be holy because God is holy (1 Pet. 1:16). The call to live holy lives is so persistent across the pages of Scripture that I am often surprised at how little attention is given to it in much Christian preaching and teaching. In the Sermon on the Mount, we are told "blessed are those who hunger and thirst for righteousness, for they shall be satisfied" (Matt. 5:6 ESV). In Romans 12:1–2, Paul exhorts the church, "Therefore, brothers and sisters, in view of the mercies of God, I urge you to present your bodies as a living sacrifice, holy and pleasing to God; this is your true worship. Do not be conformed to this age, but be transformed by the renewing of your mind, so that you may discern what is the good, pleasing, and perfect will of God." In 1 Peter 2, the apostle Peter tells a group of Christians who are already experiencing some kind of persecution,

> Therefore, rid yourselves of all malice, all deceit, hypocrisy, envy, and all slander. Like newborn infants, desire the pure milk of the word, so that by it you may grow up into your salvation, if you have tasted that the Lord is good. As you come to him, a living stone—rejected by people but chosen and honored by God—you yourselves, as living stones, a spiritual house, are being built to be a holy priesthood to offer spiritual sacrifices acceptable to God through Jesus Christ. (1 Pet. 2:1–5)

I find that some remain confused about God's call on His people to become holy. Why does God desire for us to be holy? As we read through the book of Exodus, for example, we are struck by the story of God's deliverance and redemption, but we stall out once we get to all those pesky laws God gives His people at Mt. Sinai. Why does God care what His people eat, what they drink, where they go, what they do? God provides instruction toward holiness because God knows our habits will either form us toward fellowship with life or form us toward fellowship with death. Sandpaper is rough to the touch, but it makes things smooth. Silk is soft, but it won't work out any splinters. God's call on His people to live holy lives often confronts us, but it is the kind confrontation of a master carpenter creating a more beautiful piece. Shaping us into that which is fitting, into that which is good.

Why is it good to be holy? Particularly if the pursuit of holiness requires sacrifice. Consider for a moment what the author of Hebrews says, "Pursue peace with everyone, and holiness—without it no one will see the Lord" (12:14). What do we need to be if we hope to see the Lord? We must be holy. We will not behold the blessed presence of God forever if we have not become like God. We must be holy to spend forever in delighting fellowship with the Holy One.

As I have searched God's Word for the best single sentence summary to capture the hope and calling of holiness, I find myself coming back time and time again to Hebrews 10:14 (ESV), "For by a single offering he has perfected for all time those who are being sanctified." Here we find the tension between positional and practical holiness. Positionally, all believers are perfectly holy in Christ. A Christian is someone who has received Christ's righteousness by grace through faith in Christ. As those united to the Holy One, God now declares us holy because we are in Christ. But practically, we are still working out our holiness. We are perfected, but we are still being sanctified, or becoming more and more like the

Holy One. This process is ongoing. It will not be finished until we reach the glory of heaven. Even then, we will still be "transformed from one degree of glory to another."

Behold/Become

If God's holiness is His utterly unique perfections, purity, power, and presence, then how can we become holy? Our pursuit of holiness will never result in us becoming God, but it can result in us becoming increasingly like God in our character and behavior. In truth, this isn't just an invitation from God; it's an expectation.

By beholding God's perfections, we are confronted with His limitlessness and our limits. Holiness begins with confessing that there is absolutely a perfect God and we are not Him. We can't pursue holiness if we live in defiance of creaturely limits. The impact of sin has left us thinking, feeling, and acting in a way that consistently seeks to elevate ourselves above God.

In beholding God's purity, we are confronted by His righteousness and our wickedness. God declares us holy in Christ, but we are to live with a spirit of ongoing repentance for the ways we fail God and others. Every week in worship at our church, just before we receive the Lord's Supper, we confess: "Most merciful God, we confess that we have sinned against you in thought, word, and deed, by what we have done, and by what we have left undone. We have not loved you with our whole heart; we have not loved our neighbors as ourselves. We are truly sorry and we humbly repent. For the sake of your Son Jesus Christ, have mercy on us and forgive us; that we may delight in your will, and walk in your ways, to the glory of your Name. Amen."[16] We dare not presume upon the holy grace of God, we want to walk with "broken and contrite" (Ps. 51:17 ESV) hearts as we acknowledge our need for grace and mercy. We can do this with full confidence that "if we confess our sins, he is faithful and righteous to forgive us our sins and to cleanse us from all unrighteousness" (1 John 1:9).

As we behold God's power we are confronted by His strength and our weakness. We are not able to obey God by our own power. We have to work and toil with the energy He supplies (Col. 1:29). Apart from His Spirit working in and through us, we are unable to walk obediently in His ways. It doesn't matter how polished the exterior of a car is if it has no engine. If the interior is empty of the strength and power of the Lord, we aren't able to go anywhere.

We encounter God's power, purity, and perfections as we encounter His presence. This has been the story all along. As God's people are pulled into the orbit of God's holy presence, all of their life must change. God forms us for fellowship and He forms us through fellowship. It is His presence that shapes us, but we must be shaped to enter into His presence. Obedience to God's commands is not required of Christians, but it is expected. After Paul unveils the sweet summary of the good news in Ephesians 2:1–9, he concludes with, "For we are his workmanship, created in Christ Jesus for good works, which God prepared ahead of time for us to do" (v. 10). We have been created in Christ Jesus for obedience to God's good ways.

When we choose to walk in obedience to God's ways, we can become holy in our practice. Our habits—what we actually do with our bodies, desires, and resources—can either draw us closer or push us further away from increasing conformity to the holiness of God and alignment with His design for His people. The Law of Moses, the teaching ministry of Jesus, the Wisdom Literature of the Bible, and the gospel application of the Epistles all demonstrate that after God delivers His people from the power of sin by grace through faith, He begins to direct them away from sin and toward grace-filled obedience.

We were created to reflect God's image to the world. As we become "new creations" in Christ Jesus, we are filled with the Spirit of God so that we can do just that: reflect the purity, perfections, power, and presence of God to the world. Our obedience is aimed at glorifying God, encouraging the faith of the church, and bearing witness to the Lord's character and works in front of a watching world. If our habits and behavior aren't reshaped and formed by God, our witness concerning God will lack purpose, power, and persuasion.

Reflect: What has been the most persistent sin struggle in your life with God?

Discuss: Why is it better to not sin? What joy does sin disrupt?

Practice: Make time to pray with a trustworthy brother or sister in Christ and ask them to pray specifically that you would "be holy as God is holy."

CHAPTER 9

What Do We Talk About?

"All authority has been given to me in heaven and on earth. Go, therefore, and make disciples of all nations, baptizing them in the name of the Father and of the Son and of the Holy Spirit, teaching them to observe everything I have commanded you. And remember, I am with you always, to the end of the age."
Matthew 28:18–20

If you and I hung out for a few hours, you'd probably hear me talk about Jesus, my wife, my daughter, Bob Dylan, jiu-jitsu, whatever fiction book I am reading, and the last concert I attended. Not always in that order. I wonder what I'd hear from you? What are you passionate about? Chances are that whatever you are most passionate about is what you end up proclaiming. You may be really into a style of exercise, or you may be a huge fan of a specific artist. You might be perfecting your sourdough, or you might not be able to get enough time on your grill in the backyard.

We talk about what we treasure. We proclaim our passions. What has our love will direct our language. Don't believe me? Jesus said it like this, "A good person produces good out of the good stored up in his heart. An evil person produces evil out of the evil stored up in his heart, for his mouth speaks from the overflow of his heart" (Luke 6:45). Are you going to debate Jesus? Pro tip: Never try to win an argument against Jesus. He can make donkeys talk, rocks cry out, and big fish swallow you. It's not a fair fight.

Let me say it this way: you will be a missionary for whatever has captured your heart. As Christians, we are a people who have been welcomed into the blessed presence of God by grace through faith in Christ. This is the fundamental reality of our life and the New Testament assumes that if we have been welcomed into God's kingdom, we will become witnesses to God's glory. Having seen the glory of God in the gospel, we are compelled to speak of the glory of God in the gospel.

In Deuteronomy 6, right after we are given the great command, God tells His people: "These words that I am giving you today are to be in your heart. Repeat them to your children. Talk about them when you sit in your house and when you walk along the road, when you lie down and when you get up. Bind them as a sign on your hand and let them be a symbol on your forehead. Write them on the doorposts of your house and on your city gates" (vv. 6–9). From the very first moment God's people are commanded to love God above all other things; they are commanded to share this message with everyone else.

And why wouldn't they? Israel has just been rescued from hundreds of years of enslavement. It's not a stretch to say that it is the most significant blessing they had yet received. They had seen God's power demonstrated to accomplish their deliverance and now God was telling them to declare that to the world. Consider that this is similar to what the disciples of Christ are told after He has brought an even greater deliverance through the cross and the empty tomb. Jesus gathers His people and tells them: "All authority has been given to me in heaven and on earth. Go, therefore, and make disciples of all nations, baptizing them in the name of the Father and of the Son and of the Holy Spirit, teaching them to observe everything I have commanded you. And remember, I am with you always, to the end of the age" (Matt. 28:18–20).

There is a flow throughout the story of Scripture: God's people find themselves in desperate need. God intervenes to deliver His people. God's people are to respond to this by declaring the greatness of God's character and works to the world around them. Deliverance precedes declaration. This is the proper response to God's redemption, but too often, God's people receive the wonders of God's works, but fail to testify to them with their words. The formative practice of evangelism is when God's people begin to publicly witness to the wondrous works of God. It is the public proclamation of our praise; it is telling the world why we give thanks to God.

Whatever has your worship will have your witness. The gospel is the good news that God has invited us into salvation in Christ Jesus. The New Testament presupposes that as we come to receive this glorious grace, we will become proclaimers of the message. As we behold that God is gracious, we will become people who invite others to encounter the grace of God.

A Missionary God

When you hear the word *missionary*, you probably imagine someone who is carrying a message about God. We don't often think of God Himself as a missionary, but He is. Throughout God's Word we uncover a missionary God who is determined to bring good news of His grace and victory to the world. Scripture itself is a work of the missionary God: God wrote a book to tell us who He is, who we are, and what He has done, is doing, and will do.

In Genesis 3:15, God promises Adam and Eve that one day a Savior would come to crush the work of the serpent. In Genesis 15, God makes a covenant with Abraham laying out for him exactly what He will do to redeem Abraham's descendants. Before God sends Moses into Egypt with His power and the plagues, He tells Moses in Exodus 6 how and why He will rescue His people Israel. The prophets receive very specific promises concerning God's coming Messiah, hundreds and thousands of years before He arrives.

God proclaims God. God tells of Himself. He doesn't just accomplish our salvation; He is the foremost announcer of this salvation. John 1 uses the language of "Word of God" to describe the Son of God, Jesus Christ, as it introduces the story of the incarnation. Jesus Himself, immediately following His baptism and triumph over Satan in the wilderness, goes out into the world to "preach, 'Repent, because the kingdom of heaven has come near'" (Matt. 4:17). When the Father and Son send the Holy Spirit at Pentecost, the Spirit comes upon them so that they may "receive power . . . and you will be my witnesses in Jerusalem, in all Judea and Samaria, and to the ends of the earth" (Acts 1:8).

The Father sends the Son to seek and save His people. The Father and the Son send the Spirit to empower God's people to proclaim God's Word and works to the world. Scripture is the living voice of God declaring the gospel right now, the story of His work of redemption in history, and the prophecy of His future fulfillment of all His promises. We are a missionary people because our God is a missionary God. Our witness is rooted in His witness. Our proclamation is anchored in His proclamation. We bring the gospel to the world because He has brought it to us.

A Missionary People

My daughter's favorite movie will always be the last one we watched. We are just at that age right now. Ask her a year from now and you will get a different answer. She is always going to be excited to tell you how the next movie she will see is the best movie ever. She is a missionary. A born proclaimer ready to tell you what has captured her imagination. Don't judge her too quickly. We are all like this. We are all evangelists for whatever has hooked our hearts.

We are a sent people. This isn't because we have been given a mission by God, but because we have been united to the sent Savior and empowered by the sending Spirit. Our mission isn't merely tied to a commission given by Christ, it has become our identity because we have entered into union with Christ. We often think of gospel proclamation as only preaching the gospel to those who need to hear it in order to experience salvation. That is certainly a piece of living as a missionary people, but it is not the whole project. Sharing the gospel involves encouragement, equipping, and evangelism.

Gospel encouragement is the practice of applying the gospel to the lives of our family in Christ. Consider for a moment how much time Paul spends preaching and communicating the gospel in his letters to churches. Before he shifts to telling them how to live, He tells them what God has done in Christ. Over and over again, Paul's letters show us the structure of the Christian life: Remember who you are in Christ AND then go and live in light of that new reality. In a culture full of good *advice*, Christians are entrusted with the good news of the gospel.

Gospel equipping is the practice of articulating the story and beliefs of the gospel in order to instruct. We don't just need to be encouraged by what God has done, we need to be able to articulate it and defend it. When Peter writes to the scattered Christians enduring persecution, he tells them, "But even if you should suffer for righteousness, you are blessed. Do not fear them or be intimidated, but in your hearts regard Christ the Lord as holy, ready at any time to give a defense to anyone who asks you for a reason for the hope that is in you. Yet do this with gentleness and reverence, keeping a clear conscience, so that when you are accused, those who disparage your good conduct in Christ will be put to shame" (1 Pet. 3:14–16). Peter gives these Christians gospel-equipping in order for them to be able to articulate and defend the true gospel. Why does Jude write his letter? "Dear friends, although I was eager to write you about the salvation we share, I found it necessary to write, appealing to you to contend for the faith that was delivered to the saints once for all" (Jude 3).

Gospel evangelism is the practice of sharing the gospel with those who stand under the judgment of God and are in need of salvation, and I believe that gospel evangelism is one of the most neglected formative practices in the Christian life. We can think of a hundred reasons to delay or deny God's clear command to bring the good news of the gospel to those around us. It is often fear that holds us back: fear of embarrassment, fear of rejection, or fear of failing. For many of us, shame keeps us silent. We are ashamed for how we have lived or are living in the eyes of those around us who need the gospel message. But these lies actually put the focus on us, when God's invitation is to behold His grace in Christ. As we receive this grace again and again, our evangelism is reshaped from a "have to do" to a "get to do." Consider Paul's reflection in Romans 10: "How, then, can they call on him they have not believed in? And how can they believe without hearing about him? And how can they hear without a preacher? And how can they preach unless they are sent? As it is written: How beautiful are the feet of those who bring good news. But not all obeyed the gospel. For Isaiah says, Lord, who has believed our message? So faith comes from what is heard, and what is heard comes through the message about Christ" (vv. 14–17).

Paul's logic is simple. Someone brought the gospel to you. Who will you bring the gospel to? Thank God that He sent someone to practice gospel evangelism with you and me. Will the story stop with us? Will we keep silent what God has called us to speak? The grace of God has been given to us as a gift that we might give it away freely to the world. We have been invited into fellowship with God, we now invite others to "taste and see" what we have beheld (Ps. 34). To hold back God's message of salvation is to elevate our fears and shame around evangelism over our vision of God's grace for us in Christ.

Behold/Become

I was in percussion in middle school. It wasn't cool. I thought being in percussion meant I could act like a drummer in a rock band. Instead, I was saddled with this large keyboard (imagine a fancier xylophone). This fancy xylophone was expensive, so we borrowed one from a family friend and my parents gave me firm instructions: Do not break this instrument. So, I broke it. On purpose. By throwing it across the front yard to make my friends laugh.

I opened up the case that night and saw it broken in half. I just knew that I was in for the grounding of a lifetime. That night at dinner I told my mom and dad. They were upset, rightfully so. I was grounded from video games and told that I would likely have to pay to have it fixed or replaced. That night I went to bed angsty and frustrated. I was so entitled and immature that I was angry because not only did I have to play such a dumb instrument, but now I was going to have to pay for it?! How unfair was that? Never mind that it was entirely my fault.

I woke up in the middle of the night and I couldn't sleep, so I went into the kitchen to get a glass of water. I saw a light on in the family laundry room, so I peeked through the crack in the door and saw my father on his knees fixing the keyboard with glue. It was a picture of grace. It was good news. I had made a mistake, something needed to be fixed. It was entirely my fault, and yet, I was shown grace.

That's what grace does. It changes us. It transforms us. When we encounter the grace of forgiveness and fellowship, the proper response is to share it with those around us. To tell the story again and again. When we hold back the good news of the gospel, we are in danger of becoming like the "unforgiving servant" or the person who hides their lamp. When we behold the God who invites us into salvation, we become people who invite others to encounter God.

Reflect: What are the 2–3 temptations or fears that hold you back from inviting others to encounter the God who has forgiven you?

Discuss: Who shared the gospel with you? Who was the person who invited you to behold the God who is gracious for the first time?

Practice: Identify one non-Christian adult peer in your life. Begin to pray for their salvation and make plans to share the gospel with them and invite them to follow Jesus in the next three months.

CHAPTER 10

What Do We Give Our Time To?

"Pursue the well-being of the city I have deported you to. Pray to the LORD on its behalf, for when it thrives, you will thrive."
Jeremiah 29:7

We all have a drawer in our house that is a complete mess. In my house, that drawer is in the kitchen. We even call it the "junk drawer." Need a pen, check the junk drawer. Looking for a rubber band, check the junk drawer. Where did you put that water bill? Check the junk drawer. The birthday card from your daughter you said you'd keep forever? Probably in the junk drawer.

Maybe for you it's not a drawer—it's a closet, it's the shed in the back, the garage you keep promising you are going to clean out. Listen, no judgment here. Clutter begets clutter.

Junk seems to pile up faster than we can clean it out. But what would happen if that junk drawer took over the whole house? What if it spilled out into the neighborhood? What if it covered your city? At some point that quirky little junk drawer would become quite a big problem.

You're thinking: *Are you about to tell me that keeping a tidy house is crucial for my Christian formation?* Not quite. But one crucial piece of our journey to look more and more like God is learning how to be people who create, cultivate, and care for what has been entrusted to us. This is called *stewardship.* Stewards are those who have embraced God's call to be agents of good order.

And while this call to stewardship doesn't mean that God will judge our dirty houses, it is a significant part of *having our heart, mind, and strength transformed by God the Father, in Christ Jesus, through the power and presence of the Holy Spirit at work in all the ordinary affairs of our life*. The call to care for what God entrusts to us has far too often been treated outside of the topic of Christian formation. But this is a mistake. When God created Adam and Eve, He provided them with instruction on what they were to do. This is often referred to as the cultural mandate.

In Genesis 1:27–31 we read,

> So God created man
> in his own image;

> he created him in the image of God;
> he created them male and female.
>
> God blessed them, and God said to them, "Be fruitful, multiply, fill the earth, and subdue it. Rule the fish of the sea, the birds of the sky, and every creature that crawls on the earth." God also said, "Look, I have given you every seed-bearing plant on the surface of the entire earth and every tree whose fruit contains seed. This will be food for you, for all the wildlife of the earth, for every bird of the sky, and for every creature that crawls on the earth—everything having the breath of life in it—I have given every green plant for food." And it was so. God saw all that he had made, and it was very good indeed. Evening came and then morning: the sixth day.

Image-bearers of God are told to reflect God's image and practice His purposes in the world by multiplying, cultivating, and subduing. God created a good world that was marked by order, peace, and purpose. It belonged to Him, but now He was entrusting its care to His people. It seems to me that if stewardship was crucial to God's original mandate to His people, it should be pivotal to our pursuit of becoming more like God. We must behold the good God who created a good world so that we can become wise stewards.

God Is Good

Good is one of those words that we use so casually that it has almost lost all impact. We use the word to acknowledge our agreement, we use the word to describe something we believe is morally right, we use the word to describe the tastiness of a taco. So, it would be easy for us to pass right over any significance when the Bible refers to the "goodness of God."

The Psalms are packed full of testimony that God is good:

> Taste and see that the Lord is good. How happy is the person who takes refuge in him! (Ps. 34:8)

> Enter his gates with thanksgiving and his courts with praise. Give thanks to him and bless his name. For the Lord is good, and his faithful love endures forever; his faithfulness, through all generations. (Ps. 100:4–5)

But what does it mean to say that God is good? "God is good" means that He is morally perfect. There is no corruption in God. Not only does God only do good, *God defines what good is.* God has never made a mistake and God will never do that which is evil. Not only is He morally perfect, He is absolutely trustworthy. God doesn't lie. He speaks the truth because He is truth. We can trust Him because He will never change His mind.

To say that God is "good" also means that He is beneficial. He is good *for* us. He is man's "highest good." But unlike broccoli or beets, He is both nutritious (good for us) and delicious (satisfying). God isn't just what we most deeply need, He's what we most desperately desire, even if we are not aware that He is the solution to that desire. God's goodness is also seen in that He is whole, lacking nothing. He is self-sufficient, self-existent, and self-satisfied. He is not chaos or chaotic; He isn't shifting or changing; He is not divided in any way against Himself. Every other earthly good is but a shadow of the substance of God's delighting goodness. My daughter has plastic food that we use to play "cooking" in her room. Those plastic foods typically end up in or very nearly in mouths. You'll believe me when I tell you that they aren't tasty. Earthly goods are like those plastic foods compared with the real goodness that is found in God and God alone. He is the fullness of what is good, not a reflection.

Our world was designed to reflect the goodness of God. All throughout Genesis 1, we hear God's pronouncement of "good" over what He has made. Creation was good in that it was well-ordered, whole, beautiful, and full of purpose. Contrary to other ancient creation stories, the story of

Scripture tells the true story of a world that comes into being because of an abundance of good found in God, rather than as a response to some desperate need or as a random pouring out of disordered violence.

The world God creates is designed to be a habitat for formative fellowship. As we live in God's good world, we are to form it in keeping with the character and designs of God. As we enjoy loving fellowship with God and with other image-bearers, we are to continually be formed to the image of Christ, formed for even deeper fellowship. God's design is that we would multiply image bearers; we would stretch the garden temple over the whole of the world; and we would care for what He entrusted to us. A life of meaningful worship, work, and wonder lived in God's blessed presence. Sacred stewardship in God's good ways is our commission. Even in the midst of a world now broken by sin, it remains a crucial part of our calling.

We Are Stewards, Not Owners

I don't treat hotel rooms like I treat my home. I bet you don't either. At home, I don't throw the towels on the bathroom floor when I'm done with them. I typically make my own bed. I don't leave trash sitting on the nightstand. We know that a hotel room isn't our home, so we don't pretend that it is.

Many Christians view this world the same way. They treat it like a hotel room. They think this earth is temporary, but heaven is forever, and in one sense, that's true. Heaven is forever, but heaven is forever *here*. When we read the end of the story in Revelation 21–22, we discover that heaven descends to earth, where God's people spend forever in His presence reflecting His purposes. Earth is not tossed out like yesterday's trash, it is renewed and restored, made newly hospitable for the fullness of God's presence.

This world doesn't belong to us. We don't own this world; we are stewards of it. We aren't in control; we are caretakers. The earth is not a hotel room; it's our forever home. It just needs to be dramatically remodeled. God places Adam and Eve in the garden and He commissions them with the task of ordering and cultivating His good world. The design was for Adam and Eve to stretch Eden, through multiplication and cultivation, over the whole world. Even though this mission has been disrupted by sin, it is still central to what God calls His people to do. We have been created to cultivate and as we steward God's world, He shapes and forms us more and more into His image.

Created to Cultivate

You and I were created to cultivate. We are, as some have said, "sub-creators." One of the central ways we reflect God is by creating. Now our task of creation is different from God's work of creating. God creates from nothing. We create using what God has already provided. We grow tired in the work of creating and cultivating, but God never tires. Our imaginations are limited, but God's imagination has no limits. The work of cultivation is central to God's original commission for His people in the garden and there is no reason to think it is not significant to our formation in His likeness. I want to address three ways we engage in the formative work of cultivating God's world: our vocations, our multiplication, and our pursuit of the common good.

The word *vocation* comes from the Latin word for "calling." We often think of our vocations as our jobs or careers, but really the concept of calling is both under and beyond any specific job title or career. Work is not a post-fall reality. God ordained work as one of the ways we were designed and purposed to reflect His image in the world. This work has been disrupted by the consequences of sin (Gen. 3:17–19), but its original purpose has not been destroyed. The vocation of every Christian is to "do it from the heart, as something done for the Lord" (Col. 3:23). Accountants reflect God's good design by bringing order to what could be chaos, nurses reflect God's goodness by tending to the hurts and wounds of a broken world, stay-at-home-parents reflect God's goodness by nurturing young life. God has "called" us to cultivate His world in keeping with His goodness and good design. Our vocations present opportunities to do this in the ordinary schedules and activities of our lives.

Part of that original mandate was a call to "be fruitful and multiply" (Gen. 1:28). We must understand that the simplest reading of this commission is that God is calling Adam and Eve to have and raise children. We want to dignify what Scripture dignifies and we discover from the beginning to the end of God's story that God views children as a blessing from the Lord. At the same time, we don't want to deify what Scripture dignifies. That is to construct an idol. For many, having children is not viable or is not congruent with their current stage of life. How do these people pursue faithfulness to this call? In a broken world, where not everything is as it should be, Christians can embody the call to "be fruitful and multiply" by having children, fostering children, adopting children, serving families who have, discipling children, and supporting an ethic of life in their communities. No Christian is exempt from the call to reflect God's goodness and steward His world through multiplication, but it won't always look identical for all of us.

One of the ways we can spend our time cultivating God's good world is by pursuing the common good. Our world has been broken by sin, but Christians are people who behold the good God who created a good world. As we see Him above and throughout a world marred by unrighteousness, we can bring His goodness to bear on that world by advocating for, celebrating, and investing in common good initiatives. In light of the gospel, Paul will tell the church in Ephesus, "Pay careful attention, then, to how you walk—not as unwise people but as wise—making the most of the time, because the days are evil" (Eph. 5:15–16). The way we spend our time should be marked by the wisdom of God. As we do so, we are able to redeem the time. One of the principal ways we seek the common good is by exercising love toward our enemies. This is precisely what Jesus says in Matthew 5:43–48. In these few short verses Jesus connects the love of enemies with the justice of God to ordain the sun to rise and fall and the rain to come and go for both the "righteous and the unrighteous." If we love our enemies, we will seek their good even if they hate us. In this way, Jesus repeats the wisdom of the prophet Jeremiah, who tells God's people in exile to "Pursue the well-being of the city I have deported you to. Pray to the LORD on its behalf, for when it thrives, you will thrive" (Jer. 29:7).

Become/Behold

What do you do when you are trying to put together a puzzle? You look at the picture on the box. By seeing the picture, we can begin to grasp where to put the pieces. We can only become good stewards of God's world when we behold the goodness of God and His designs. There is no hope that we can be helpful in putting all the pieces in their proper place if we take our eyes off of the One who purposed the picture itself.

As we engage in our vocations, in multiplication, and in pursuing the common good, God uses these practices to shape and form us into His likeness. But that's not all. He also uses them to shape and form His world. We are to go out into the dark and desolate places and perform the acts of His kingdom. We are sub-creators, called to reflect our creator God as we cultivate and innovate in His world. Every act of God-glorifying creation and cultivation proclaiming the truth, beauty, and goodness of the Creator Himself. This work will not go unopposed, but it will end undefeated.

Reflect: What's one area of the world around you that feels desperately "broken"? If you were going to image God in that space, what would that look like?

Discuss: How do most people believe that the world changes? Do people feel like they can bring meaningful change to the world around them? Why or why not?

Try: Take fifteen minutes to answer this question: "How does my vocation give me regular opportunities to reflect God's goodness in the world?"

CHAPTER 11

Who Is Our Enemy?

Therefore, submit to God. Resist the devil, and he will flee from you.
James 4:7 ESV

It's a normal part of growing up to have an enemy. You may call them a bully, rival, or jerk. I called my arch-nemesis "Vaughn" because that was his name. Vaughn was bigger than me. A lot bigger. And he liked to bully me. I could live with the bullying, but one day Vaughn moved from bully to enemy. How? He stole my best baseball card after gym class in fifth grade. I could never forgive him. For years I would just look at Vaughn and think, *One day I'll get you back.*

Years after Vaughn's theft, I was packing up my room to head off to college. As I dug through the mess in my cluttered closet to get what I needed, I picked up an old shoebox stuffed with junk to throw in the trash. As I went to drop it in the bag, I noticed that stuck to the bottom was the very card

Vaughn had stolen. Vaughn may have been a bully, but he was never really my arch-nemesis. That doesn't mean I didn't have an enemy. It just wasn't who I thought it was.

I know why books on Christian formation don't often talk about spiritual warfare. It feels strange and weird. We'd rather not imagine that part of the Christian journey involves following God in a world where evil spiritual forces are active and eager to "steal and kill and destroy" (John 10:10), but this is the world we live in. There is a great Enemy of God. His power has been defeated, but his presence still remains.

We should not be surprised to discover that spiritual warfare is a significant part of the journey of Christian formation, because battle with the Enemy is a significant part of the story of Christ. Right after Jesus's baptism, with the magnificent declaration that Christ is the Father's "Beloved Son, with whom He is well pleased," Jesus heads off into the wilderness for a showdown with Satan. Adam failed in the good garden, but Christ is victorious even in the midst of the weary wilderness. Christ's victory over Satan begins with the wilderness temptation, but is showcased throughout the Gospels as Jesus casts out demons, heals the sick, teaches truth, and eventually, puts death to death in His crucifixion and resurrection.

In Colossians 2, Paul exhorts the church, ". . . as you received Christ Jesus the Lord, so walk in him" (v. 6 ESV). But what does he ground this appeal in? The good news of Christ's victory: "And when you were dead in trespasses and in the uncircumcision of your flesh, he made you alive with him and forgave us all our trespasses. He erased the certificate of debt, with its obligations, that was against us and opposed to us, and has taken it away by nailing it to the cross. He disarmed the rulers and authorities and disgraced them publicly; he triumphed over them in him" (Col. 2:13–15). When Paul uses the phrase "rulers and authorities," he isn't talking about the Jewish or Gentile political and religious leaders. This phrase is used to refer to the spiritual forces of evil, to what he would call "powers" in Romans 8.

All throughout the New Testament we are reminded that it is because God is victorious that we are victorious. His victory becomes ours in Christ Jesus. We will encounter opposition from the spiritual forces of evil: torment, temptation, affliction, and persecution. But there is good news: as we behold the God of victory, we become more than conquerors.

God Is Victorious

When two opponents of equal strength square off in competition or battle, we call that a "fair fight." Make no mistake: God's battle with Satan has never been, is not now, nor will it ever be a fair fight. God is the Sovereign Creator and Lord of all created things. His power, position, and glory have never been challenged by an enemy of equal strength, because there is no enemy of equal strength. Jesus's temptation in the wilderness is a picture of perfect obedience in the face of human temptation;it is not a demonstration that God is subject to Satan.

The victory of God over Satan is demonstrated across the story of the Bible:

- God exposes Satan's lies (Genesis 3).
- God overthrows a serpent king in the Exodus event (Exodus 1–19).
- God alone can permit Satan's testing of Job (Job 1).
- Jesus triumphs over Satan to begin His public ministry (Matthew 4).
- Jesus casts out demons in His healing and deliverance ministry (Matthew 8 and Mark 5).
- Jesus tells Peter that Satan "demanded to have" him, but Jesus wouldn't allow it (Luke 22:31 ESV).
- On the cross of Christ, Jesus, "disarmed the rulers and authorities and disgraced them publicly; he triumphed over them in him" (Col. 2:15).
- Revelation is a whole book about the victory of God over evil, sin, Satan, and death.

God is sovereign over Satan. Scripture leaves absolutely no doubt about this. In the work of Christ Jesus, God has conquered the power of Satan and all evil spiritual forces in the heavenly places. While their power is gone, their presence remains. But a day is coming when the very presence of Satan and all evil spiritual forces will be consigned to hell forever. The victory of God is as sure and certain as the empty tomb. It is rock solid.

We Have an Enemy

So if God has conquered the power of Satan in the work of Christ, then I guess that means we have nothing and no one to fight against. If Satan has already been defeated, there is no fight left, right? Not exactly. The clear testimony of Scripture is that while the power of Satan has been removed, his presence still haunts this world. We are still under attack, but our Enemy now attacks us even as he retreats from the victory of God.

When we say that Satan's power has been destroyed, we mean that he has been disarmed by the life and work of Christ Jesus. He can tempt, he can threaten, but he cannot possess God's people and he cannot steal us from our home with God in Christ Jesus. As Paul writes in Romans 8:37–39, "No, in all these things we are more than conquerors through him who loved us. For I am persuaded that neither death nor life, nor angels nor rulers, nor things present nor things to come, nor powers, nor height nor depth, nor any other created thing will be able to separate us from the love of God that is in Christ Jesus our Lord."

Evil powers still oppose us, but we no longer have to fear that they can overcome us. They can't. They no longer have the power. This doesn't mean there is not still a battle to fight. The author of Romans 8 is the same who wrote Ephesians 6:11–13, 18:

> Put on the full armor of God so that you can stand against the schemes of the devil. For our struggle is not against flesh and blood, but against the rulers, against the authorities, against the cosmic powers of this darkness, against evil, spiritual forces in the heavens. For this reason take up the full armor of God, so that you may be able to resist in the evil day, and having prepared everything, to take your stand. . . . Pray at all times in the Spirit with every prayer and request, and stay alert with all perseverance and intercession for all the saints.

We are called to love our enemies, but we are also told to stand against the Enemy. Our battle is not against other people, it's against the "cosmic powers of this darkness." Who are these cosmic powers? They are the spiritual forces of evil and they actively oppose Christ's people.

The journey of Christian formation is *having our heart, mind, and strength transformed by God the Father, in Christ Jesus, through the power and presence of the Holy Spirit at work in all the ordinary affairs of our life.* In this journey we encounter resistance in the form of indwelling sin, the brokenness of the world, and yes, the active opposition of evil spiritual forces. We really should not be surprised to find that the very same opposition Christ encountered in living His life will be experienced by us as we look to be conformed into His image. Does this mean that every spiritual setback, trial, or hurdle the Christian experiences is the direct result of spiritual warfare? No. But it does mean that the Christian should expect to encounter spiritual opposition as they look to have their heart, mind, and strength transformed by God.

Notice what Paul's battle strategy is in Ephesians 6. Where does Paul root the believer's strength to stand fast against these spiritual forces? How do we overcome the attacks of Satan? By beholding God. The armor of God is rooted in the works of God. Truth, righteousness, gospel peace, faith, salvation, and the Word of God all are anchored in what God has done in Christ Jesus. We can fasten the belt of truth, because we have encountered the one who was "full of grace and truth" (John 1:14). We can be covered by righteousness because God "made the one who did not know sin to be sin for us, so that in him we might become the righteousness of God" (2 Cor. 5:21). Each piece of the armor of God is anchored in the person and work of Christ. As we behold the victory of God in Christ, we can become victorious in the battle against the "cosmic powers of darkness."

We Have a Confidence

We all know that David killed Goliath, but do you remember what happens right after the giant falls? After David beheads Goliath (yes, that happens), it says, "When the Philistines saw that their hero was dead, they fled. The men of Israel and Judah rallied, shouting their battle cry, and chased the Philistines to the entrance of the valley and to the gates of Ekron" (1 Sam. 17:51–52). The Israelites had been too scared to attack, but once Goliath was defeated, they rushed headlong into the battle and overwhelmingly defeated their enemies. What changed? They saw an unlikely hero defeat an "unbeatable" enemy.

The Christian approaches spiritual warfare with the same confidence. The great Enemy has been felled. His head has been crushed (Gen. 3:15). We are invited to enter into the battle knowing that the war has already been won. We can fight the daily skirmishes against evil with a new confidence. A confidence that is rooted in Christ's victory, not our ability. When we are tempted, we can refrain from sinning. When we are tormented, we can hold to the embers of resurrection hope. When it seems evil has won the day, we can know that a day of final judgment is approaching.

We have the confidence to enter into places of darkness, death, and despair and "practice resurrection."[17] This means that we can call evil what it is, without submitting ourselves to its power and influence. As James says, "Submit yourselves therefore to God. Resist the devil, and he will flee from you" (James 4:7 ESV). Satan does not flee because we are strong, but because we have become identified with the great Champion. Our confidence is rooted in the power of God and we can stand as conquerors because we are in Christ Jesus. The victory of Christ is given over to us—so that even when we feel like big losers, we are actually beloved victors.

We become "more than conquerors" (Rom. 8:37) in and through Jesus Christ. As we behold the God of victory in Christ, His victory becomes our own. His triumph is our treasure in the face of Satan's temptation. As one of the old catechisms so wonderfully said, "I am not my own, but belong with body and soul, both in life and in death, to my faithful Savior Jesus Christ. He has fully paid for all my sins with his precious blood, and *has set me free from all the power of the devil.*"[18]

Behold/Become

The journey of Christian formation is opposed, but it isn't hopeless. "Be sober-minded; be watchful. Your adversary the devil prowls around like a roaring lion, seeking someone to devour" (1 Pet. 5:8 ESV). We are to "resist him" (v. 9). Our resistance is rooted in reflecting on what God has already accomplished in Christ Jesus: "The sting of death is sin, and the power of sin is the law. But thanks be to God, who gives us the victory through our Lord Jesus Christ!" (1 Cor. 15:56–57).

How do we resist the temptations and torments of Satan and his forces? By beholding the victory of God. We look upon God and His wonderful works more than we look at ourselves. We boldly resist the temptations of Satan, knowing that God has already overcome his power and disarmed him. Every time you say "no" to that which is evil and wicked, you defy Satan and you deepen your fellowship with the God who has conquered him. When we give into temptation, we re-submit ourselves to the "ruler of the power of the air, the spirit now working in the disobedient" (Eph. 2:2). This is who we once were outside of Christ, but in Christ Jesus, we have been rescued "from the domain of darkness and transferred us into the kingdom of the Son he loves" (Col. 1:13).

The principal way that we battle with the Enemy and his forces is through prayer. When Paul instructs the Ephesian Christians to battle against Satan and evil spiritual forces, he begins by telling them to receive and put on the armor of God. Each piece of armor is rooted in the character and works of God. He is telling them: Behold the God who brings you peace! Behold the God who clothes you in His righteousness! Behold the God who gives you truth! Behold the God who grants you salvation! Behold the God whose faithfulness grounds your faith! On the foundation of this beholding, what are the Christians in Ephesus to do? Battle in prayer. Equipped in the armor of God they are to "Pray at all times in the Spirit with every prayer and request, and stay alert with all perseverance and intercession for all the saints" (Eph. 6:18).

Our victory is given to us in Christ. God is victorious over the Enemy. It is by beholding His victory that we become more than conquerors. Conquerors who practice intercessory prayer in the confidence that God is "able to do above and beyond all that we ask or think according to the power that works in us" (Eph. 3:20). This is the hope that anchors our hearts in the heat of battle against Satan and his devices. The hope that Satan's power has been destroyed by the God of victory and that one day, hopefully soon (*maranatha*), his very presence will be confined to judgment forever.

Reflect: On a scale from 1–10, with "1" being not ever and "10" being all the time, how often do you consider that the difficulty or wicked temptation you are experiencing in your life as a follower of Jesus is a result of evil spiritual forces?

Discuss: How do we imagine Satan and evil spiritual forces? What does Scripture say about satanic and demonic activity?

Practice: Memorize Colossians 2:15, "He disarmed the rulers and authorities and disgraced them publicly; he triumphed over them in him."

CHAPTER 12

Where Is Our Hope?

"Look, I am making everything new."
Revelation 21:5

I stood in line outside the bookstore with a bunch of other nerds. We were waiting for midnight so that we could be the first people to buy the last book in a series that had gripped our imagination for over a decade. As we waited, a truck pulled around the corner of the parking lot with some rowdy teenagers in the back. As they pulled the truck up to this long line of bookworms, one of the boys pulled out a megaphone and shouted out the end of the story. He revealed a giant secret. He spoiled the ending. There was mayhem. Well, as much mayhem as a group of midnight book buyers can cause.

Nobody likes a spoiler. But the Christian story gets better when you spoil the ending. As we discover what God is going to do in the future, the way we live in the present is re-formed and reshaped by this coming day. Like the Israelites after David defeated Goliath, we can chase down the enemies of God's kingdom because we know the true King has come, defeated the giant, and is coming again.

In 1 Corinthians 13, the apostle Paul tells us that "For now we see only a reflection as in a mirror, but then face to face. Now I know in part, but then I will know fully, as I am fully known. Now these three remain: faith, hope, and love—but the greatest of these is love" (vv. 12–13). We began back at the beginning of this book in our exploration of the formative practices with love and now we turn our attention to hope.

Hope is native to the human heart—though it is often misplaced. All sorts of things will hook and lead our hopes. We will root our hope in money, the next day off, a good night's sleep, a better tomorrow. We really don't want to believe that things are hopeless, but in our endeavor to find something that can carry the hopes of our hurting hearts, we end up discouraged because our hopes are too heavy for the shoulders of anyone and anything but God.

Hope is further challenged by looking at the world around us. A world that seems perpetually marked by wickedness, evil, and death. Whether it's seeing an aging face in the mirror or another headline of despair online, we can begin to believe that hope is a liar and a cheat. Life under the sun can sometimes feel like living through an unending night. We end up asking: Is it naive to hope?

God invites us into something real: a real expectancy in a world full of false promises; a resurrection realism in a world haunted by the presence of a defeated death. When we look ahead, to the end of the story, we hear the whispers of a day when all things will be made new. As we behold the coming King, we become people of *honest* hope.

The Coming King

When I was a new Christian, I didn't want Jesus to come back. At least, not anytime soon. Don't judge me too quickly. I think a lot of Christians, at least when they are being honest, have at one time or another had a similar thought. I had all sorts of plans, dreams, and hopes. Jesus coming back soon was going to mess all that up. I knew heaven was going to be better than this world and was certainly better than the alternative, but I really wanted to go to Disney World. My cousin had told me they had a roller coaster that was INDOORS. That was pretty heavenly for a ten-year-old's imagination.

I couldn't see it fully then and sometimes I forget it now, but it is good news that the King is coming back. We live in what theologians refer to as the *already/not yet*: our time is the time between the first coming of the Son of God and His second and final return. In this age, we are left looking back to remember what God has done and looking forward to what He has promised to do.

It is indisputable that the Bible connects hope with the second coming of Christ. Romans 8:18, 22–25 provides an extended meditation on this hope:

> For I consider that the sufferings of this present time are not worth comparing with the glory that is going to be revealed to us. . . . For we know that the whole creation has been groaning together with labor pains until now. Not only that, but we ourselves who have the Spirit as the firstfruits—we also groan within ourselves, eagerly waiting for adoption, the redemption of our bodies. Now in this hope we were saved, but hope that is seen is not hope, because who hopes for what he sees? Now if we hope for what we do not see, we eagerly wait for it with patience.

This is called eschatological hope. Eschatology means *consideration of last things.* When we consider what the Bible says about the end of the world, the proper response is *hope*. Hope that God is going to return to make all things right, for good, forever. This hope is grounded in the resurrection of Christ, which is precisely the point Paul makes in 1 Corinthians 15.

Because we can look back on the empty tomb, we can look forward to the coming King.

Christian hope is not fueled by speculation about the details of the end of days. We do not hope in what we guess, we hope in the promises of God. We hope for the day when we see "a new heaven and a new earth . . . the holy city, the new Jerusalem, coming down out of heaven from God" (Rev. 21:1–2). We hope to hear the voice of the Lord from the throne saying, "Look, I am making everything new" (v. 5).

False Hope(s)

I remember buying my first piece of gold. I couldn't believe they were selling it in the museum's gift shop. I ran up to my dad and said, "Can you believe they are selling gold for five dollars?" I didn't understand his smirk then, but I do now. Of course he knew it was fool's gold, but to a six-year-old on a summer vacation, it seemed real to me.

In this age between the times, this *already/not yet*, we are surrounded by people selling hope. Unfortunately, they turn out to be worse than five-dollar fakes. We are tempted to accept them because we are desperate for hope. Christian or not, it is easy for despair to take root and leave us so needy for good news that we'd drink sea water to try and quench the thirst.

All false stories have something to say about hope. Progressivism proclaims hope in social advancement. Digital utopianism encourages hope in technological achievement. Consumerism wants you to buy hope with the next purchase. Individualism believes that you really just need to hope in your hustle. The cynic says hope is a lie. For hope to be genuine it has to do two things: correctly identify the problem and point toward a real solution. False stories can't do this; they incorrectly identify the problem with the world, incorrectly identify the solution, or both.

When Paul is confronted by the risen Christ in Acts 9 at his conversion, he is awakened to the false story he has been living in. Paul firmly believes that he is doing what is good and right by chasing after followers of Jesus in order to crush this movement of "the way" (Acts 9). His conversion on the road to Damascus doesn't simply lead to his salvation, but to the renewal of his imagination. The persecutor who presides over the death of the first martyr, would become the prophet of a new resurrection hope—a resurrection hope for all of God's people rooted in the very same Christ he had been persecuting. When articulating the Christian hope, the Bible never paints a picture that is dismissive over death. Rather, it invites us into an "honest hope."

Honest Hope

We all know an optimist. Someone who seems to always be able to see the sunny side of things. If you can't think of an optimist or you are annoyed that I am doing that thing again where I use a simple observation or story to introduce a larger point, you are likely a pessimist. If that's you, you're in good company, because I too am afflicted with the "glass half empty" sensibility. I have always been one of those people who has a hard time hoping. I wouldn't say that I am dour or perpetually sad, but I often assume the worst will happen. I can be having a wonderful day and see a minor cloud on the horizon and immediately fixate on the approaching storm.

Christian hope isn't peppy optimism, but neither is Christian honesty perpetual pessimism. When we behold the coming King, we are welcomed into an honest hope. A hope that can say, "The last enemy to be destroyed is death" (1 Cor. 15:26 ESV). Christian hope isn't naive; it is willing to look into the darkness, death, and despair of this world caught between the *already/not yet* and to whisper: Maranatha, Lord Jesus, come.

I think it's fair to say that some of us live on the honesty side of the spectrum and others live on the hope side. We need each other. We have to be reminded that while the world is often dark, there is a Light that it cannot extinguish (John 1:1–18). We need someone to tell us that the hope of heaven is real even when it feels like all we see is death and suffering. We need the psalmist's question: "Why, my soul, are you so dejected? Why are you in such turmoil? Put your hope in God, for I will still praise him, my Savior and my God" (Ps. 42:5). An honest hope recognizes both brokenness and beauty. An honest hope can say: The King is coming *and* I hope He comes soon because I am sick of a sin-sick world.

We often think of hope as a feeling. Because we are embodied creatures with souls, we can often feel hope or hopelessness. Our feelings are part of who we are created to be, but they are not always the most reliable thermometer for what is true. Whether we are disposed to feel hope or not, we can practice hope. Like the psalmist says in Psalm 130, "I wait for the LORD, my soul waits, and in his word I put my hope" (v. 5 ESV). Hope is looking to the horizon, even in the dead of night, knowing that the sun will break the darkness.

In 1 Peter, we see Peter ground Christian hope in the glory and promise of the coming King:

> Blessed be the God and Father of our Lord Jesus Christ. Because of his great mercy he has given us new birth into a living hope through the resurrection of Jesus Christ from the dead and into an inheritance that is imperishable, undefiled, and unfading, kept in heaven for you. You are being guarded by

> God's power through faith for a salvation that is ready to be revealed in the last time. You rejoice in this, even though now for a short time, if necessary, you suffer grief in various trials so that the proven character of your faith—more valuable than gold which, though perishable, is refined by fire—may result in praise, glory, and honor at the revelation of Jesus Christ. Though you have not seen him, you love him; though not seeing him now, you believe in him, and you rejoice with inexpressible and glorious joy, because you are receiving the goal of your faith, the salvation of your souls. (1 Pet. 1:3–9)

We have received a "living hope" through the resurrection of Jesus Christ. But where does this hope direct us? It directs us toward a salvation that is "ready to be revealed in the last time." Peter appeals to his audience that this hope is their grounds for rejoicing, even in the midst of their sufferings. Notice that Peter doesn't try to minimize their sorrow and suffering. He doesn't rationalize it away. He knows his audience is suffering for the sake of the faith, but they can still rejoice. Why? Because the "revelation of Jesus Christ" is coming. A day is coming when their faith will be made sight.

Behold/Become

There once was a successful Christian lawyer. He and his wife lived near Chicago with their five children. Then he lost almost everything in the great Chicago fire. Around the same time, his four-year-old son died from fever. Two years later, his wife and four daughters set sail to cross the Atlantic, only to collide with another ship. His wife was rescued, but his four daughters died that day at sea. As he crossed the Atlantic to get to his wife, his only surviving family member, he said to himself, “It is well; the will of God be done.” He would later use that phrase as the foundation for a hymn that would go on to be one of the most treasured hymns of the Christian tradition: “It Is Well with My Soul.”

Horatio Spafford had become a man of honest hope. He had lost almost everything and yet he could sing, “But, Lord, ’tis for Thee, for Thy coming we wait, the sky, not the grave is our goal; Oh, trump of the angel! Oh, voice of the Lord! Blessed hope, blessed rest of my soul! And Lord, haste the day when the faith shall be sight, the clouds be rolled back as a scroll; The trump shall resound, and the Lord shall descend, Even so, it is well with my soul.”[19] He beheld the coming King. He looked toward the end of the story and he saw the glory of a King who makes all things new.

One day all the sad things will be made untrue. We will hear a loud voice from a throne descending and God will "wipe away every tear from our eyes. Death will be no more; grief, crying, and pain will be no more, because the previous things have passed away" (Rev. 21:4). The foretaste that we have had of the promised fellowship will finally arrive in fullness.

Reflect: What things you have placed your hope in that ended up disappointing?

Discuss: How does where we place our hope change the way we live?

Practice: Draw a picture with your nondominant hand of what it feels like when you feel hopeless. I know this sounds strange. But when you try to draw this with your non-dominant, it's going to activate a feeling of helplessness. You aren't as strong or skilled with that hand. And we can only begin to be honest about our hope or hopelessness, when we acknowledge how helpless we often feel. After you draw the picture, take time to pray and ask the Lord to give you an "honest hope."

CONCLUSION

Beholding What We Become

I had seen babies. Like other polite people, I had looked down and smiled at babies and then told their parents, "They are so cute!" For the most part, I never lied. Okay, maybe a handful of times I was bending the truth to the point of breaking. I had seen many babies, but it wasn't until I met my daughter that I *beheld* a baby. And it changed me.

Even this morning as she crawled into our bed for a mercifully lazy Saturday with no plans, my eyes were closed, but I lay there beholding my wife and daughter. Filled with joy, thanksgiving, praise. My eyes were closed, but they had my full attention.

Jesus tells the people, "Blessed are the pure in heart, for they will see God" (Matt. 5:8). Why is this such a great promise? Because beholding God is receiving joy. Beholding

God is delight. Beholding God is what will satisfy the deepest desire of all our hearts, whether we know it or not. Every other joy we chase, every other satisfaction we hunt, every other desire that simmers to the surface is a whisper that beneath them all eternity sits in our hearts longing for a glimpse of the Eternal One.

Why is the journey of Christian formation worth it? It will be costly; it will be challenging. It will require discipline and it will require self-denial. We are tired of ordinary lives, and walking with God is anything but ordinary. We are full of competing desires for good things and bad things, and the good only wins when our eyes are fixed on Jesus and our lives are being shaped into His form. The journey is worth it because He is the prize.

Why practice sacrificial love? Why give our attention to God instead of the crowds on social media? Why pin our hope in heaven's glory and not the next vacation?

For a glimpse of God. A glimpse that will one day become more than just looking through a keyhole. We pursue deep spiritual formation so that we might enter into deeper fellowship with God. Like a thimble of water transformed into an ocean, one day our faith will be made sight and our beholding no longer hindered by the weight of the world, the sins of the flesh, and the heartache of exile. The beatific vision, the beholding of the Blessed One that blesses, is our why. And it's coming for all of God's people. Every day between now and then for God's people is the opportunity to enjoy a foretaste of that future forever.

Formative practices like prayer, reading God's Word, Sabbath rest, corporate worship, obedience, and evangelism are invitations to behold God. And as we behold God, we will become like Him. This journey doesn't end when we arrive at heaven's gates. The journey of Christian formation is a forever journey. As Paul writes in 2 Corinthians, "And we all, with unveiled face, beholding the glory of the Lord, are being transformed into the same image from one degree of glory to another. For this comes from the Lord who is the Spirit" (3:18 ESV).

In C. S. Lewis's *Mere Christianity*, he captures the hope of the formative practices of the Christian life:

> If you want to get warm you must stand near the fire: if you want to be wet you must get into the water. If you want joy, power, peace, eternal life, you must get close to, or even into, the thing that has them.[20]

As we make our home with God in Christ, God begins to form and shape us, refashioning the way we live so that we may receive what He has already declared is fully ours in Christ. Christian formation begins the moment that the Christian life starts, but it never ends. You and I are invited to behold the glory of God. Here and now we may catch mere tastes, glimpses, whispers; but we are headed into a forever home where the glory of the Lord will light up the world like the sun. As we behold His glory, we will be transformed. Beholding forever. Becoming forever.

We will never reach the bottom of what glory there is to behold in God. We shall see Him, but we will never be able to contain Him. And just as there is no bottom to His glory, there will be no finish line of our formation. As we behold more and more of His glory, we will become more and more a reflection of His presence and purposes, drawn deeper into fellowship with the God whom we behold.

We have been changed, we are being changed, we will be changed. We are becoming what we behold. Hear the voice of Jesus, "Look, I am making everything new" (Rev. 21:5). He has, He is, and He will. And until the fullness of time arrives, we "seek his face" (Ps. 27:8), knowing that one day soon, the veil will be removed. We will see God and be seen by Him. The blessing of beholding what we will become. Forever.

Acknowledgments

It seems like the acknowledgments section for these books is a list of the "usual suspects."

I am immensely grateful for my friends, J. T. English and Jen Wilkin, who have been such fruitful partners in this endeavor for more than a decade. The book would not have been possible without the tireless editing effort of Mary Wiley, trust me when I tell you that anything bad or unhelpful in this book was something that Mary tried to convince me to cut or change. Anything good she made better. The entire team over at B&H is outstanding.

I have to thank Erik Wolgemuth, my agent, who continues to simply be the best guy in Christian publishing. I am grateful for the encouragement and support of the pastors of Mosaic Church in Richardson, Texas, with whom I co-labored in prayer during the writing of this book to see God form His people in this community.

Thanks to the hundreds of participants in the Training Program or Forge Program over the years who have helped sharpen the content of this book with their wonderful questions and contributions.

I am forever indebted to Dr. David Naugle for teaching me how to think. And I will never miss an opportunity to honor Joseph and Cheryl Worley, my father and mother, for whom there are simply no words to describe my gratitude.

To my wife Lauren: I love you so much. Thank you for such enduring support through my peaks and valleys. You are a treasure. I promise I will run out of words eventually.

To my daughter Lydia: Thank you for always asking me to play during my writing sessions. Playing with you is more fun than writing. I can't wait to read what you write next.

About the Author

Kyle Worley is a pastor, teacher, author, and podcast host. He is the host of the *Knowing Faith* podcast with Jen Wilkin and J. T. English that reaches millions of listeners each year. He is the author of *Home with God: Our Union with Christ* (B&H) and one of the founding partners of Training the Church. You can find out more about him at KyleWorley.net or follow him on social media @kyleworley.

Notes

1. Andy Crouch, *The Life We're Looking For: Reclaiming Relationship in a Technological World* (New York: Convergent, 2022), 11.

2. Here I am using the subtitle to J. R. R. Tolkien's *The Hobbit* and a line from C. S. Lewis's *The Final Battle.*

3. Al Wolters, *Creation Regained: Biblical Basics for a Reformational Worldview* (Grand Rapids: Eerdmans, 1985), 72–73.

4. For more on these false stories, see J. T. English's *Remember and Rehearse: An Invitation to Participate in God's Story* (Brentwood, TN: B&H, 2025), pages 14–25.

5. Alasdair MacIntyre, *After Virtue: A Study in Moral Theory* (Notre Dame, IN: University of Notre Dame Press, 2007), 216.

6. Kyle Worley, *Home with God: Our Union with Christ* (Brentwood, TN: B&H, 2025).

7. Augustine, *On Christian Doctrine*, I. 27–28.

8. Robert Louis Wilken, *The Spirit of Early Christian Thought: Seeking the Face of God* (New Haven, CT: Yale University Press, 2003), 50.

9. Mary Oliver, *Upstream: Selected Essays* (New York: Penguin, 2016), 8.

10. Tim Keller, @timothykellernyc, X, February 23, 2015, https://x.com/timkellernyc/status/569890726349307904?lang=en.

11. Eugene H. Peterson, *Answering God: The Psalms as Tools for Prayer* (New York: HarperOne, 1991), 35.

12. Donald S. Whitney, *Praying the Bible* (Wheaton, IL: Crossway, 2015).

13. C. S. Lewis, *The Magician's Nephew* from The Chronicles of Narnia (New York: HarperCollins, 2001), 62.

14. G. K. Beale, *We Become What We Worship: A Biblical Theology of Idolatry* (Downers Grove, IL: IVP Academic, 2008), 16.

15. "Downer Episode," *Bojack Horseman*, season 1, episode 11 (Tornante Company), Netflix, 2014.

16. Episcopal Church, *The Book of Common Prayer and Administration of the Sacraments and Other Rites and Ceremonies of the Church: Together with the Psalter or Psalms of David According to the Use of the Episcopal Church* (Seabury Press, 1979).

17. Wendell Berry, "Manifesto: The Mad Farmer Liberation Front," *The Selected Poems of Wendell Berry* (Berkeley, CA: Counterpoint, 1999), 88.

18. George W. Richards, *The Heidelberg Catechism: Historical and Doctrinal Studies* (Publication and Sunday School Board of the Reformed Church in the United States, 1913), emphasis added.

19. Horatio G. Spafford, "It Is Well with My Soul," public domain.

20. C. S. Lewis, *Mere Christianity* (San Francisco: HarperCollins, 1952), 176.

ALSO AVAILABLE

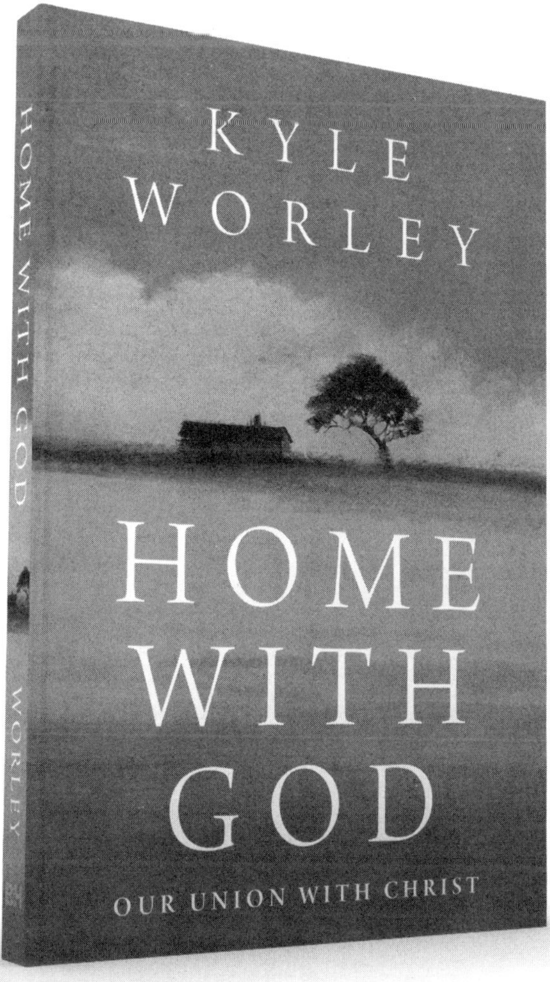

Available wherever books are sold

B&H PUBLISHING

Deep
Discipleship
TORY | BELIEF | FORMATION